T0098225

RAND

National Security Research Division

Australian Foreign and Defense Policy in the Wake of the 1999/2000 East Timor Intervention

PETER CHALK

Supported by the
Smith Richardson Foundation

The research described in this report was sponsored by the Smith Richardson Foundation. The research was conducted through the International Security and Defense Policy Center (ISDPC) of RAND's National Security Research Division (NSRD).

Library of Congress Cataloging-in-Publication Data

Chalk, Peter.
    Australian foreign and defense policy in the wake of the 1999/2000 East Timor intervention / Peter Chalk.
       p. cm.
     "MR-1409."
     Includes bibliographical references.
     ISBN 0-8330-3044-2
     1. Australia—Military policy. 2. Australia—Foreign relations—1945– 3. Timor Timur (Indonesia)—Foreign relations—Australia. 4. Australia—Foreign relations—Indonesia—Timor Timur I. Rand Corporation. II. Title.

UA870 .C483 2001
327.940598—dc21

2001048135

Published 2001 by RAND
1700 Main Street, P.O. Box 2138, Santa Monica, CA 90407-2138
1200 South Hayes Street, Arlington, VA 22202-5050
201 North Craig Street, Suite 102, Pittsburgh, PA 15213
RAND URL: http://www.rand.org/
To order RAND documents or to obtain additional information, contact Distribution Services: Telephone: (310) 451-7002; Fax: (310) 451-6915; Email: order@rand.org

In late 1999, Australia committed to the country's most significant external military operation since the Vietnam War—the intervention to stem the violence and bloodshed that was unleashed following East Timor's August 1999 vote to separate from Indonesia. This book addresses the conceptual basis that has largely underscored Australian foreign and defense policy and examines how the intervention in East Timor has had an impact on this paradigmatic framework. It analyzes the implications of the International Peacekeeping Force for East Timor (INTERFET) for Canberra's future defense and security planning, and assesses what this means for wider United States geostrategic interests.

This book should be of interest to policymakers concerned with defense and security issues in Southeast Asia and the evolving nature of the Australia–United States alliance.

The research for this study was funded by a grant from the Smith Richardson Foundation as part of its International Security and Foreign Policy Program. This research was conducted within the International Security and Defense Policy Center (ISDPC) of RAND's National Security Research Division (NSRD). NSRD conducts research and analysis for a broad range of clients, including the U.S. Department of Defense, allied foreign governments, the intelligence community, and foundations.

CONTENTS

An enduring challenge that Australia has confronted since attainment of state-hood in 1901 is how to reconcile its Western origins with its Asian geography in creating a viable security identity. During the Cold War, this issue was generally framed in the context of the wider geopolitical standoff that was taking place between the United States and Soviet Union. However, in the more fluid international political environment since the fall of the Berlin Wall in 1989, it is the notion of comprehensive engagement that has largely been used to define and specify Australia's role in this part of the world. This orientation does not connote the idea of "belonging" to Southeast Asia; rather, it expresses a desire to forge a diverse and substantive array of linkages with the countries of the region in a spirit of partnership and mutual respect.

Indonesia has been critical to the success of comprehensive engagement. The Republic is not only Australia's largest and most important regional neighbor, its preeminent position in organizations such as the Association of Southeast Asian Nations (ASEAN) ensures that the country will have a key voice in endorsing (or rejecting) Canberra's wider regional engagement efforts. To this end, intensive efforts have been made to establish and cement comprehensive aid, investment, security, and political ties with Jakarta.

East Timor has functioned as something of a test for the notion of Australian regional engagement and especially the country's long-standing policy of seeking closer relations with Indonesia. To be sure, Jakarta's 1975 invasion and subsequent annexation of the territory runs counter to many of the fundamental beliefs held by Australians regarding good governance and humanitarian values. However, there has also been a general acceptance of the status quo in East Timor as the only basis for fruitful cooperation with Indonesia and, thereby, identification with Southeast Asia. Emblematic of this, throughout the 1980s and most of the 1990s (when the focus on comprehensive engagement was paramount), successive Australian leaders and politicians were prepared to acquiesce in Jakarta's integration of the East Timor province and often violent suppression of Timorese pro-independence dissent.

It was only in late 1998 that a shift began to occur in this accommodationist policy. In particular, Australia began to exhibit a predilection for far more forceful diplomacy, perhaps best reflected by the lead role Canberra assumed in the armed United Nations International Peacekeeping Force for East Timor (INTERFET) that was dispatched in September 1999. Several factors appear to have played a role in encouraging this policy departure. Notable among them were (1) government assessments that suggested Indonesia could simultaneously handle its own transition to democracy while dealing with the loss of East Timor; (2) personal interjections by the Australian foreign minister, Alexander Downer, who strongly identified with the self-determination aspirations of the East Timorese people; (3) the totally unexpected decision by Indonesian President B. J. Habibie to allow a "popular consultation"[1] in the province of East Timor to determine local support for a wider autonomy package for the Timorese; and (4) growing uncertainty, disorder, and violence in East Timor itself, which became particularly marked between July and September 1999.

The most immediate impact of Australia's actions in East Timor has been felt in terms of the country's relationship with Indonesia, which is currently the worst it has been for three decades. Restoring some degree of stability to the bilateral partnership will take time and require deft management. The key for Canberra over the next few years will be to shape policies that constructively build on those diplomatic openings that do exist, while moving to ensure that potential pitfalls do not escalate to the point of assuming unwarranted significance and importance on the bilateral agenda.

To this end Australia should do the following:

- Play a constructive role in undertaking initiatives to bolster East Timorese self-sufficiency and ensuring the territory's long-term viability. This will contribute to peace and security along Indonesia's southern rim and help to ensure that East Timor acts as a bridge (rather than an obstacle) to relations between Canberra and Jakarta within the wider Southeast Asian community.

- Promote more intensive (and constructive) person-to-person links through tourism and educational exchanges, and by fostering an active program of "track-two" diplomacy.[2]

---

[1] The action that resulted in the separation of East Timor from Indonesia was officially termed a "popular consultation" by the United Nations.

[2] *Track-two diplomacy* is conducted by academics, regional experts, and state and country officials acting in a private capacity. It is meant to inform policy and decisionmaking at the official governmental level (known as *track-one diplomacy*) by providing for a free and frank exchange of

- Contribute to Indonesia's economic development and restructuring, both directly by providing aid and assistance and indirectly by acting as an intermediary between Jakarta and international financial institutions.

- Embrace the various moderate factions that continue to hold sway in Indonesia, especially in terms of emphasizing the many mutual benefits that can result from bilateral functional contacts and cooperation.

- Categorically demonstrate support for Indonesia's continued territorial integrity by developing effective confidence-building measures (CBMs) for Irian Jaya and Aceh, the two most restive provinces in the Indonesian Republic today.

- Facilitate human development, professionalism, and cooperation with the Indonesian military by (1) maintaining and expanding periodic educational activities and staff college-level exchanges, and (2) collaborating to address "soft," nontraditional military threats of mutual concern such as piracy and unregulated population movements.

Beyond the relationship with Indonesia, the East Timor intervention had a decisive impact on Australian defense planning and thinking. In particular, it provided a compelling rationale for creating a new type of defense structure that would allow quick and decisive deployments to contain complex humanitarian emergency situations whenever they arose in or near to the country's principal areas of strategic concern (the South Pacific and Southeast Asia). The blueprint for achieving this long-run reconfiguration is set out in the White Paper on Australian Defence 2000 (discussed in Chapter Five of this report). This plan implies a reordering of priorities, away from the maintenance of high-tech, conventional sea and air platforms to the creation of highly mobile land forces that can operate in defense of Australia as well as undertake lower-level missions in regional "hot spots."

Several problems exist with Defence 2000, however, which not only reflect a residual preoccupation with traditional defense postures but, more important, suggest a level of "schizophrenic" thinking in long-term strategic planning. In particular, the White Paper largely leaves unanswered the fundamental question of the way in which the Australian Defence Force (ADF) should be evolving: toward a low-end peacekeeping configuration or a high-tech entity that keeps abreast of the revolution in military affairs (RMA). Moreover, the Defence 2000 Review[3] fails to elucidate whether Canberra should be preparing its forces to meet proximate regional threats or whether the emphasis should be

---

ideas and allowing what might otherwise be overly sensitive issues (in an official forum) to be discussed and debated.

[3]Defence 2000 Review and 2000 Defence White Paper are used interchangeably in this report.

on configuring ADF assets so that they can be more readily integrated into wider Southeast Asian defense and security arrangements.

Two primary findings can be extrapolated from the analysis of the Defence 2000 Review presented in this report:

- First, the open-ended nature of the White Paper's planning commitments has led to the danger that a resource-deprived differential force structure will be created, which is lacking at both the high and low ends of the defense spectrum.

- Second, the ambiguity that underscores much of the review's language has fed into a somewhat obfuscated Southeast Asian policy and generated largely unfounded expectations of what Australia is able (and willing) to do in terms of its alliance commitments with the United States and the associated contributions to coalition warfare.

ACKNOWLEDGMENTS

The author wishes to express his thanks to the Smith Richardson Foundation for its interest and assistance in funding this project. A debt of appreciation is also owed to James Clad and James Haseman, both of whom provided highly useful and insightful comments on the draft version of this study.

Several people were integral to the completion of this research. A particular note of thanks is extended to the following:

- Dr. Kusnanto Anggoro, Center for Political and Regional Studies, Indonesian Institute of Sciences (PPW-LIPI), Jakarta, Indonesia

- Dr. Greg Barton, Deakin University, Melbourne, Australia

- Dr. Anthony Bergin, Australian Defence Studies Centre (ADSC), Canberra, Australia

- Andrew Byrne, Department of Defence, Canberra, Australia

- Dr. James Cotton, Australian Defence Force Academy (ADFA), Canberra, Australia

- Alan Dupont, Strategic and Defence Studies Centre (SDSC), Canberra, Australia

- David Fetter, U.S. State Department (Australia Desk), Washington, D.C.

- Adrienne Jackson, Australian Embassy, Washington, D.C.

- Dr. Suzaine Kadir, National University of Singapore, Singapore

- John McFarlane, Australian Defence Force Academy (ADFA), Canberra, Australia

- Brigadier Brian Millen, Australian Embassy, Jakarta, Indonesia

- Dr. Paul Monk, La Trobe University, Melbourne, Australia

- Greg Moriarty, Australian Embassy, Jakarta, Indonesia

- Steven Mull, U.S. Embassy, Jakarta, Indonesia

- Major Ken Norman, Department of Defence, Canberra, Australia

- Captain David Ramsay, Australian Embassy, Jakarta, Indonesia

- Dr. Muna Riefqi, Research Institute for Democracy and Peace (RIDèP), Jakarta, Indonesia

- Sara Rye, Australian Embassy, Jakarta, Indonesia

- Dr. Leonard Sebastian, Institute of Southeast Asian Studies (ISEAS), Singapore

- Gordon Stirling, U.S. State Department (Australia Desk), Washington, D.C.

- Dr. Hermawan Sulistyo, Research Institute for Democracy and Peace (RIDeP), Jakarta, Indonesia

- Andrew Tan, Institute of Southeast Asian Studies (ISEAS), Singapore

- Professor William Tow, University of Queensland, Brisbane, Australia

- Bruce Vaughn, Australian Embassy, Washington, D.C.

- Dr. Stewart Woodman, Australian Defence Force Academy (ADFA), Canberra, Australia

- Ganewati Wuryandari, Center for Political and Regional Studies, Indonesian Institute of Sciences (PPW-LIPI), Jakarta, Indonesia.

Needless to say, any errors or omissions are solely the responsibility of the author.

ACRONYMS AND ABBREVIATIONS

ABRI	Angkatan Bersenjata Republik Indonesia
ADF	Australian Defence Force
ADFA	Australian Defence Force Academy
ADSC	Australian Defence Studies Centre
AFTA	ASEAN Free Trade Area
AII	Australia-Indonesia Institute
AIMF	Australia-Indonesia Ministerial Forum
AMS	Agreement on Mutual Security
ANU	Australian National University
ANZAC	Australia–New Zealand Agreement (Canberra Pact)
ANZUS	Australia–New Zealand–United States
APCSS	Asia Pacific Center for Security Studies
APEC	Asia-Pacific Economic Cooperation
Apodeti	Association for the Integration of Timor into Indonesia
ASEAN	Association of Southeast Asian Nations
BRIMOB	Indonesian Police Mobile Brigades
CAPP	Center for Asia-Pacific Policy
CBM	Confidence-building measure
CEPT	Common Effective Preferential Tariff

CIA   Central Intelligence Agency

CSCA   Conference on Security and Cooperation in Asia

CSCAP   Council for Security Cooperation in the Asia Pacific

DFAT   Department of Foreign Affairs and Trade

EU   European Union

FPDA   Five Powers Defence Arrangements

Fretelin   Revolutionary Front for an Independent East Timor

GAM   Gerakan Aceh Merdeka

GIC   Good international citizenship

GNP   Gross National Product

IADS   Integrated Air Defense System

IASFOR   Indonesia-Australia Forum

IDSS   Institute for Defense and Strategic Studies

IGGI   Inter-Governmental Group on Indonesia

IMF   International Monetary Fund

INTERFET   International Peacekeeping Force for East Timor

ISEAS   Institute of Southeast Asian Studies

JORN   Jindalee Operational Network

KOSTRAD   Indonesian Army Strategic Reserve Force

MFA   Armed Forces Movement

NMD   National Missile Defense

NRO   National Reconnaissance Office

NUS   National University of Singapore

OPM   Free Papua Movement

PKI   Indonesian Communist Party

PNG   Papua New Guinea

PRC	People's Republic of China
RIDèP	Research Institute for Democracy and Peace
RMA	Revolution in military affairs
SAS	Special Air Service
SDSC	Strategic and Defence Studies Centre
SEATO	Southeast Asia Treaty Organization
SF	Special Forces
SIGINT	Signals intelligence
SLOC	Sea-lane of communication
SOG	Special Operations Group
TGZCT	Timor Gap Zone of Cooperation Treaty
TNI	Tentara Nasional Indonesia
UDT	Timorese Democratic Union
UK	United Kingdom
UN	United Nations
UNAMET	United Nations Assistance Mission in East Timor
UNTAET	United Nations Transitional Authority in East Timor
VLF	Very low frequency

In late 1999, Australia undertook a commitment to the country's most significant external military operation since the Vietnam War—the intervention to stem the violence and bloodshed that was unleashed following East Timor's August 1999 vote to separate from Indonesia. The action not only represented a major shift in Canberra's traditionally accommodationist policy toward Jakarta, which since 1976 had largely sacrificed taking a harder line on the East Timor situation for the sake of upholding the wider Indonesian relationship. The intervention also generated significant questions regarding the future direction of Australian defense policy and force restructuring, engagement with Jakarta and Southeast Asia, and the nature of the evolving strategic alliance with Washington.

An enduring challenge that Australia has confronted since attainment of statehood in 1901 is how to reconcile its Western origins with its Asian geography in creating a viable security identity. More specifically, policymakers have been faced with an ongoing "distant looks our way" dilemma in that Australia is a regionally isolated Western state, which has both fed the Australian sense of identity and contributed to its phobias. The primary way that Canberra has sought to address this issue since the end of the Cold War (prior to which its alliance with the United States was the dominant focus) has been to cultivate stable and harmonious relations with Jakarta.

The Republic of Indonesia is not only Australia's largest and most important regional neighbor, it is also the crucial state upon which wider Southeast Asian engagement has largely depended. To this end, intensive efforts have been made to establish and cement comprehensive aid, investment, security, and political ties with Jakarta, an orientation that became particularly critical under the Labor Government of Australian Prime Minister Paul Keating (1991–1995) when the partnership with Indonesia became one of Canberra's main policy priorities.

East Timor has functioned as something of a test case for the notion of regional engagement and, especially, Canberra's long-standing policy of seeking closer relations with Indonesia. Although Jakarta's annexation of the province runs counter to many of the fundamental beliefs held by Australia regarding good governance and humanitarian values, a general acceptance of the status quo in East Timor has been upheld as an important basis for cooperation with Indonesia and, thereby, identification with Southeast Asia. This accommodationist stance held true as late as 1998 after which a substantial shift began to occur in Canberra's thinking, perhaps best reflected by the lead role that Australia assumed in the International Peacekeeping Force for East Timor (INTERFET) that was dispatched in September 1999.

The intervention in East Timor carries important implications for Australia's security and defense policy in Southeast Asia, especially with regard to managing the bilateral partnership with Indonesia. Relations between Canberra and Jakarta have progressively deteriorated since the August 1999 "popular consultation" that resulted in the separation of East Timor from Indonesia and are currently the worst they have been in three decades. Very much indicative of this situation was the 1999 cancellation of the 1995 Agreement on Mutual Security (AMS), which many commentators have interpreted as effectively signaling an end to the contemporary peace dividend enjoyed by the two countries.

Whether Canberra can repair its relationship with Jakarta and convince its other northern neighbors—particularly Malaysia, which, at least under Prime Minister Mahathir Mohamad, has been highly suspicious of Australia's pro-Western disposition—that it is not about to embark on a more militaristic and (U.S.-backed) hegemonic role in regional security remains to be seen.

In addition to considerations pertaining to regional engagement, the INTERFET episode raises significant conceptual questions regarding the future of Australian defense and intelligence planning, particularly in light of the nature of the conflict in Southeast Asia, its scale and durability, the locus of future "East Timors," and the warning of conflicts erupting elsewhere that might be expected.

Above all, the INTERFET episode highlights the need for the Australian Defence Force (ADF) to move away from its current preoccupation with a divisional structure and reorganize around the concept of independent brigades and rapid reaction forces, with more emphasis on mobility and a greater reliance on tactical reserves. The extent to which this restructuring can be reconciled with the somewhat conflicting objective of remaining at the cutting edge of the revolution in military affairs (RMA)—to both ensure interoperability with the

United States and keep ahead of developments currently taking place in other Southeast Asian states—is an issue that will present acute policy challenges.

The situation in East Timor and the extent of its impact on the future direction of Australian defense and security policy are also likely to have relevance for broader United States interests. On the one hand, a more active regional role will help to offset Washington's responsibilities in Southeast Asia, something that fits well with the current Bush administration's present emphasis on reduced overseas commitments. However, if the more-active regional role comes at the expense of investments in wider force interoperability, it could well have impact on Canberra's ability (and willingness) to actively contribute to alliance operations in more-distant theaters (such as the Korean Peninsula and the Taiwan Straits), which is at odds with an equally important theme in present United States thinking—that of coalition warfare.

The research for this report proceeded in three stages:

- First, a qualitative and conceptual framework for Australian security and defense policy was established based on a survey and assessment of relevant primary and secondary source materials found in the open literature.

- Second, interviews were conducted in Australia, Indonesia, Southeast Asia, and the United States to determine the short- and long-term implications of Canberra's intervention in East Timor and how these implications have had an impact on the country's defense and foreign policy calculus.

- Third, the principal findings of the field work were integrated and incorporated into the initial literary assessment and analysis to generate a final document.

The overall aim of this report is to address the conceptual basis that has largely underscored Australian defense and security planning policy, and examine the extent to which the intervention in East Timor has had an impact on this paradigmatic framework. This report analyzes the implications of INTERFET for Canberra's future defense and security planning and assesses what they mean for wider United States geostrategic interests.

Chapter One of this report describes the principal developments that have taken place in Australian foreign and defense policy since World War II. The principal focus of the chapter is on the notion of "comprehensive engagement," the main basis upon which Canberra's regional Southeast Asian policy has rested for most of the past decade.

Chapter Two examines the key role that Indonesia has played in Australian defense and foreign policy thinking from 1945 to the present. The bilateral relationship between Jakarta and Canberra is assessed within the contextual framework established in Chapter One.

Chapter Three looks at the 1998 to 2000 intervention in East Timor. The aim of the chapter is threefold: first, to elucidate the main parameters that guided Australian policy toward the Indonesian incorporation of the province for most of the latter half of the 1990s; second, to describe Canberra's role in brokering and mediating peace talks between Jakarta and pro-independence elements in East Timor and ultimately its role in leading the INTERFET stabilization force; and third, to explain the bureaucratic and political context in which decisions to become more actively involved were made.

Chapter Four examines Australian-Indonesian relations in the wake of the East Timor intervention and assesses the prospects for future contacts between the two countries. It considers what sort of partnership is realistically feasible under present conditions and outlines basic building blocks to further bilateral cooperation and interaction. The potentially explosive issue of defense ties is also discussed and gauged in terms of the extent to which these contacts can be reinstituted.

Chapter Five analyzes the main policy implications of the 2000 Defence White Paper. It highlights several contradictions that appear to underpin this review, particularly the combined emphasis on low-tech as well as high-tech force requirements and the characterization of Southeast Asia as a region against which Australia needs to both safeguard itself and cooperatively engage. The chapter discusses the implications of these considerations for Canberra's regional policy of Asian interaction and assesses how they might have an impact on Australia's wider alliance with the United States.

Chapter One

THE HISTORY AND EVOLUTION OF AUSTRALIA'S FOREIGN POLICY IN SOUTHEAST ASIA

This chapter provides an overview of the development of Australia's foreign policy in Southeast Asia. First, I examine policy as it developed up until 1969, when the first indications of a more-independent foreign policy became more apparent. This follows with a discussion of the years from 1969 until 1991, the first year of the Labor Government of Australian Prime Minister Paul Keating. This chapter concludes with an analysis of the post–Cold War era, much of which has been concerned with forging a substantive set of political, economic, and security links with the countries of Southeast Asia.

AUSTRALIAN FOREIGN POLICY TO 1969

Ever since Australia attained independence from the United Kingdom (UK) in 1901, the federation has been faced with the challenge of reconciling its Anglo-Saxon origins with its Asian geography in creating a viable security identity. For the first 70 years of the twentieth century, Canberra sought to deal with this dilemma by fostering friendly relations with the world's major Western powers in the hope that those nations would underwrite Australia's own security interests in the Asia Pacific.

Initially, the Commonwealth looked to Great Britain to fulfill this external guarantor role. Indeed, prior to the end of World War II, foreign policy, if it existed at all, merely revolved around Australia's supporting and endorsing initiatives that came out of London. Although policymakers in Canberra were prepared to differ with the British on substantive issues such as immigration, relations with Japan, and regional security, it was always in the context of influencing Imperial policy and rarely, if ever, in support of creating independent Australian policy designs (Evans and Grant, 1995).

The slow development of an autonomous foreign policy was not due to a lack of interest in it. To the contrary, very early on, the Australian government demonstrated a keen awareness of external issues, particularly those pertaining to the Pacific region. However, Canberra's lack of power and diplomatic independence vis-à-vis Great Britain largely precluded the possibility of flexibility and influence in international affairs.

If Australia wanted to have an impact beyond its borders, even if only in its own backyard, it inevitably had to confer with London. As Evans and Grant suggest, the period from 1901 to 1939 is thus characterized not by the evolution of a foreign policy per se, but by a belief that Australian diplomacy necessarily had to be conducted, if not on behalf of, at least in conjunction with British officials (Evans and Grant, 1995, p. 21). This was perhaps no more clearly illustrated than when Australian Prime Minister Robert Gordon Menzies (1939–1941 and 1949–1966) announced war against Germany in 1939:

> It is my melancholy duty to inform you officially that in consequence of a persistence by Germany in her invasion of Poland, Great Britain has declared war upon her and that as a result, Australia is also at war.[1]

The unstated implication was that if London had become involved in a conflict of this magnitude, Canberra had a reciprocal responsibility to participate in it. Inherent in this logic was the assumption that only the UK had the wherewithal to protect Australia from the power plays of other European states (such as Germany and Russia) and Asiatic nations, and more specifically Japanese incursions from the north.

Moreover, if one looks closely at Australia's defense structure between World Wars I and II, it is clear that the government had yet to adopt an ambitious course for any kind of engagement that went beyond basic security needs. Because foreign policies were closely pegged to the UK alliance's system of imperial defense, Canberra saw little reason to maintain a strong military force or strike out on its own. The experiences of World War I in which Australia, along with New Zealand, suffered the highest proportionate casualty rate (as a percentage of its population) of any of the participants[2] further solidified this attitude and mitigated against the government pushing for a more self-reliant posture.

During the second World War, a change began to occur in the direction (although not the substance) of Australia's thinking regarding foreign policy, with Canberra increasingly looking to the United States, rather than Britain, as its external guarantor. The Japanese aggression in the Pacific proved to be a

---

[1] Menzies announcement of war, cited in Meaney, 1985.

[2] With a total population of 4 million, Australia enlisted 416,809 men to fight in World War I. Twenty percent of those combatants were killed and 45 percent were wounded. For detailed figures see Grey, 1999, pp. 15–16.

decisive factor in galvanizing this shift. The catastrophic sinking of two British warships, the HMS *Repulse* and HMS *Prince of Wales*, in December 1941,[3] and London's failure to prevent the fall of Malaya and Singapore in 1942 and, more important, preempt the Japanese attacks on the Australian coastal cities of Darwin and Broome, underscored a simple reality in Canberra: In times of global conflict, the UK's capacity to provide for Australian interests was, at best, extremely limited.[4]

The dominant role played by the Americans in the Pacific War—not the least in terms of liberating Southeast Asia from Japanese occupation—merely confirmed this perception (Evans and Grant, 1995, pp. 21–22; Brown, 1977, p. 27; Jones and Smith, 1999, p. 444). More specifically, it precipitated a growing consensus that it was the United States, and not the United Kingdom, that could best guarantee Australia's forward defense in Asia.

Whereas these changes in thinking did represent something of a watershed in terms of the evolution of Australian foreign policy, it is important to not exaggerate the extent of the change that actually occurred. Although Canberra's traditional ties with Great Britain were loosened by the experiences of World War II—which, in many ways, allowed for more freedom and flexibility in foreign policy decision-making[5]—the government's margin for maneuvering was always small and restricted by wider geostrategic imperatives. As Evans and Grant point out, Australia had merely turned from one protector to another and in many ways continued to see its own policies as intimately tied to the global objectives of major external powers (Evans and Grant, 1995, p. 22).

The context for much of Australia's post–World War II foreign policy was provided by the American doctrine of containment, which was largely precipitated first by Chairman Mao Tse-tung's victory in China in 1949 and second by the French defeat in Indochina in 1954. Drawing on U.S. President Dwight D. Eisenhower's articulation of the "domino theory," Prime Minister Menzies defined a related concept, "forward defense," committing Australia to the active preemption of Communist (and, at least initially, possible resurgent Japanese) influence in the Asia-Pacific. The linchpin of the policy was a willingness to act as the Western Bloc's primary southern "anchor" by engaging in joint actions with the United States and its major allies.

---

[3]The combined death toll from the two sinkings was 840—513 from the *Repulse* and 327 from the *Prince of Wales*.

[4]The failure of the British to prevent the nationalization of the Suez Canal in 1956 greatly endorsed this line of thinking because it further emphasized to Australia that the UK was no longer a major player on the global scene.

[5]Indicative of this greater flexibility was the decision to bring back Australian troops from Europe to help with the defense of the Pacific after the Japanese attack on Pearl Harbor in December 1941.

Thus, Canberra endorsed the Colombo Plan (a modest Asian version of Marshall Aid) in 1950, concluded the Australia–New Zealand–United States (ANZUS) Pact with Wellington and Washington in 1951 (which became the cornerstone of the country's security policy during the Cold War), and joined the Southeast Asia Treaty Organization (SEATO) in 1954. It also strongly opposed Indonesian President Sukarno's attempts to oust the Dutch from Irian Jaya—a policy that increasingly came to be defined in terms of a radical, quasi-leftist ideology on nonalignment—and worked alongside the UK during both the Malayan Emergency (1948 to 1960) as well as the undeclared "confrontation" (*konfontasi*) between Indonesia and Malaysia (1963 to 1966).

The ultimate expression of this geopolitical outlook, however, was the commitment to send combat troops to Vietnam in April 1965 to curtail what Prime Minister Menzies described as "China's drive south between the Pacific and Indian Oceans." Although this can hardly be considered a decision made completely at the behest of Washington—the war dominated Australia's domestic political scene for nearly a decade—it certainly was part of a policy framework that went beyond immediate Australian national interests (Jones and Smith, 1999, p. 444; Gelber, 1968, pp. 25–34). Indeed, expressing a logic that was remarkably reminiscent to the thinking that drove Canberra to declare war on Germany in 1939, the Australian Embassy in Washington gave the following justification for involvement in the Indochina conflict:

> Our objective should be to achieve such an habitual closeness of relations with the U.S. and sense of mutual alliance that in our time of need, after we have shown all reasonable restraint and good sense, the U.S. would have little option but to respond as we would want.[6]

AUSTRALIAN FOREIGN POLICY BETWEEN 1969 AND 1991

It was Australia's commitment to the more militant aspects of American foreign policy that first galvanized the revisionism in Canberra's own Anglo-centric bias. Disillusionment with the war in Indochina, particularly after the United States' enunciation of the Guam Doctrine, which essentially emphasized that America's allies must accept primary responsibility for their own defense,[7] generated a rising tide of nationalism within the country. This, together with a

---

[6]Minister-Counsellor Alan Renouf, quoted in Frost, 1987, p. 16.

[7]The Guam Doctrine was first announced by President Richard Nixon in July 1969 and then passed by the U.S. Congress in February 1970. It stated that whereas the United States was prepared to extend its nuclear "umbrella" to allies in the Asia-Pacific, henceforth the expectation would be for those allies to assume primary responsibility for their own defense. The doctrine essentially emerged out of growing American domestic opposition to the war in Vietnam and was an attempt to ensure that the country would not be drawn into another overseas conflict far from its own borders.

concern over Australia's general involvement in Southeast Asian political and economic affairs, precipitated a growing critique of the federation's post-1945 foreign policy agenda, which culminated in 1972 with the election of the country's first Labor government in 23 years. The new administration, under Prime Minister Gough Whitlam, immediately asserted that Australia had its own unique interests, which needed to be determined and assessed in light of the country's specific circumstances and not as part of the United States' wider global objectives (Evans and Grant, 1995, pp. 26, 326).

In line with this revised foreign policy bias, the Australian government downplayed the centrality of the American (forward defense) alliance system, placing greater emphasis on regional engagement and self-reliance (although it was not until the late 1980s and early 1990s that these concepts were fully integrated into Australian foreign policy). Canberra also reoriented aspects of its vigorous anti-Communist stance, formally recognizing North Vietnam, North Korea, and the People's Republic of China (PRC) and legally endorsing the incorporation of the Baltic States into the Soviet Union (the only democratic country to ever do so) (Jones and Smith, 1999, p. 448; O'Neill, 1973, p. 31; Sheridan, 1995, p. 7; "Defence Shift Is Overstated," 2000).

It should be noted that a number of these changes were also influenced, at least partially, by the general reordering of Southeast Asian politics following the signing of the 1973 Paris Peace Accords, which formally ended the phase of the United States' direct military involvement in the Vietnam War. Certainly nations such as Thailand, Malaysia, and New Zealand were taking similar steps in what was broadly regarded as a necessary adjustment to an altered regional geostrategic environment.

Whereas the Whitlam era played a role in revitalizing the Australian political landscape, this interlude was short-lived and as a result largely ephemeral in terms of its impact. Following the fall of Whitlam's government in 1975, the underlying pattern of Australian foreign policy quickly returned with the election of Malcolm Fraser (1975 to 1983). Although the new prime minister did not specifically set out to reverse the foreign policy initiatives of the preceding administration, he consciously reaffirmed the Australian-American alliance as a simple, cheap, and effective way of securing the country's interests in Asia (Evans and Grant, 1995, p. 27).[8]

---

[8] Fraser also reaffirmed the importance of the Australia–New Zealand Agreement (ANZAC; otherwise known as the Canberra Pact) that Canberra signed with Wellington in 1944. This accord had always been situated within the broader context of the U.S. alliance. (See Smith, Cox, and Burchill, 1997, pp. 103–104.)

Indeed, it was not until as late as the 1980s that any decisive moves were made to develop and institute a forceful and systematic policy of regional engagement. To be sure, the administration of Prime Minister Bob Hawke that governed Australia from 1983 until 1991 continued to endorse and support a vigorous United States alliance. Canberra, for instance, leveled strong criticism at New Zealand following Wellington's decision to prevent American nuclear-armed vessels from visiting its ports (which effectively ended its participation in the ANZUS alliance) asserting that this decision undermined a key pillar of peace and stability in the South Pacific (Evans and Grant, 1995, p. 29).[9] Moreover, Australia continued to host various space defense and submarine very low frequency (VLF) radio facilities for Washington, rejecting arguments that this was in any way inconsistent with the vocal position it had begun to adopt on global disarmament issues (Evans and Grant, 1995, p. 29).

However, in what was to become a precursor for the post–Cold War era, far more direct unilateral attention started to be paid to the Asia-Pacific itself. Not only did Hawke attempt to establish more integrated and substantive economic links to the north, first initiating the Asia-Pacific Economic Cooperation (APEC) process in 1989, he also sought to situate Australia as an active participant in regional middle-power diplomacy.

To a large extent, these initiatives were a byproduct of the 1987 Defence White Paper, which for the first time spelled out a coherent policy of security self-reliance (that is, non–U.S. dependent) based on sophisticated, high-end detection and strike capabilities designed to protect the "air-sea gap" to Australia's north.[10] The strategic imperative inherent in this paradigmatic shift was extremely important in that it allowed foreign ministers to think about the promotion of regional defense and stability in a more dynamic, flexible, and systematic manner than ever before (Cotton and Ravenhill, 1997, pp. 1–2; Jones and Smith, 1999, p. 450; Evans, 1989, pp. 44–45).

Nonetheless, the success of Hawke's efforts in Asia was always compromised by the continuing emphasis that his government gave to the alliance with the United States. Not only did this artificially constrain the policy "liberation" borne out of the 1987 White Paper, it also helped to create a regional percep-

---

[9]The United States actually unilaterally suspended its obligations to New Zealand after Prime Minister David Lange announced that his government would not allow entry to the USS *Buchanan* without first receiving explicit nonnuclear assurances, which was against the nuclear strategic doctrine of the U.S. Navy.

[10]It should be noted that whereas Australia was seeking to advance a more independent foreign policy line in the Asia-Pacific, many of its initiatives squared well with the needs and interests of the United States. APEC helped to advance Washington's multilateralist agenda of economic and security regionalism, while more advanced "air-sea" gap defense capabilities ensured a more-secure American ally able to act effectively within its own neighborhood.

tion, particularly evident in the rhetoric of states such as Malaysia, that the country was neither fully committed to nor an integral part of Asia. It was in this context that Mediansky wrote at the end of the 1980s not of Australia's closer regional engagement with countries in Southeast Asia but merely of its diminished regional standing (Mediansky, 1992, p. 27). In 1991, Paul Keating assumed power with a self-defined mandate to overturn the legacy of previous Canberra administrations, which had tended to emphasize Australia more as a U.S.-aligned Western country than one genuinely committed to the Asia-Pacific.

THE POST–COLD WAR ERA

During the post–Cold War era, two governments have determined Australian foreign policy: the Labor administration of Paul Keating (1991–1996) and the Liberal-Nationalist coalition of John Howard (1996–present). Although coming from different ends of the political ideological spectrum, both have consciously sought to consolidate Australia's regional position in the Asia-Pacific.

The Paul Keating Administration

Australia's geopolitical shift toward Asia undoubtedly gathered momentum from the late 1980s on. On one level, this shift in emphasis reflected the changing nature of the international states' system. The debate over whether Australia should continue to define its foreign policy in terms of the United States or on the basis of independently assessed imperatives was essentially decided thanks to the collapse of the Soviet Union and the subsequent end of the Cold War. As this new geostrategic landscape emerged, Australia found itself in a world remarkably different from the one it had occupied for the past 40 years.

No longer seeing itself as wholly dependent on the United States for protection, Australia began to more vigorously pursue the course it had tentatively started in the mid-1970s, namely, defining its own unique interests independent of traditional alliance commitments while seeking to develop a network of new regional ties. An early indication of this reoriented post–Cold War posture was the proposal for a Conference on Security and Cooperation in Asia (CSCA), which was specifically advanced as a metaphor for Asian dialogue and mutual confidence building (Evans and Grant, 1995, p. 117).[11]

---

[11]Australian policy at this time also identified with the post–Cold War aims of democratization and individual human rights, which placed the country uncomfortably in the middle of the "Asian versus Western values" debate that had begun in the early 1990s. Aware of the dangers that this position posed to the wider objective of regional engagement, Canberra opted to pursue these general goals through quiet and tacit diplomacy (as opposed to the more-strident approach the United States was emphasizing).

Just as important, however, was the influence of Paul Keating, who undertook a personal commitment to link and integrate Australia's destiny with that of the Asia-Pacific. Through a heavy program of overseas visits and by cultivating close personal partnerships with regional leaders, the prime minister set about articulating the notion of a politically and economically integrated region of which Australia was unequivocally a part (Evans and Grant, 1995, pp. 30–31; Cotton and Ravenhill, 1997, pp. 1–2). Particular emphasis was given to the relationship with Indonesia, which not only represented Canberra's logical link to Southeast Asia (given its geographic proximity) but also acted as a vital bedrock country that was critical to the maintenance of the region's wider cohesive order. The conceptual foundation upon which Keating and his foreign minister, Gareth Evans, sought to develop this vision of regional enmeshment was comprehensive engagement, which was itself based on an expanded and more-inclusive notion of security.

Comprehensive engagement was developed in the late 1980s to complement and provide added ballast to the 1987 Defence White Paper, which had shifted Canberra's policy nucleus away from its dependency on the relationship with the United States to an orientation that emphasized a more discrete and self-reliant regional focus. The intention behind this concept was not to convey the idea that Australia "naturally" belonged to Southeast Asia. Rather, it sought to engage the countries of the region in a spirit of partnership and mutual respect by forging a diverse and substantive array of cross-linkages and contacts. The long-term goal was to foster a Southeast Asian community of peace and security, of which Australia was both recognized and welcomed as an integral part, based on a shared set of common defense norms and interests.[12]

Evans enunciated the terms of comprehensive engagement in the following manner during his December 6, 1989, Statement on Australia's Regional Security:

- Building a more diverse and substantive array of linkages with the countries of Southeast Asia, so that they have an important interest in the maintenance of a positive relationship with Australia

- Continuing to support the major existing regional association, the Association of Southeast Asian Nations (ASEAN), and working with the countries of the region to shape additional regional multilateral organizations or arrangements, such as APEC, which can contribute to the social and economic evolution of the region

---

[12]For a good overview of the concept of comprehensive engagement see MacIntyre, 1991.

- Participating actively in the gradual development of a regional security community based on a sense of shared security interests[13]

- Working for the involvement of Vietnam, Cambodia, Laos, and Myanmar in the cooperative framework of regional affairs

- Recognizing that Australia, in vigorously pursuing its national interests in the region, should do so as a confident and natural partner in a common neighborhood of remarkable diversity, rather than as a cultural misfit trapped by geography (Evans, 1989, paras. 173–176).

The comprehensive engagement approach built on and expanded classical notions of military security. Similar to the divisional concept used in war, the new strategy implied a reconceptualization of security that both widened the sphere of potential threat contingencies and, in so doing, moved beyond a view of defense that focused simply on military deterrence. More specifically, it permitted greater flexibility in foreign relations by emphasizing multidimensional policies that were designed to meet the needs of several issue areas (military, diplomatic, environmental, and economic) deemed to be of common interest to all countries in Southeast Asia.

Australia's pursuit of comprehensive engagement under Prime Minister Keating was reflected by a regional foreign policy agenda that was both vigorous and proactive. In Indochina, considerable time, energy and resources were devoted to facilitating the process of national reconciliation and democratization in Cambodia. Australia worked closely with Japan, the United States, and the European Union (EU) in bringing about the negotiations that led to the 1991 Paris Peace Settlement and actively participated in the United Nations transitional authority that was subsequently dispatched to lay the groundwork for the 1993 independence elections. Canberra also played a key role in promoting economic growth and development in Cambodia as part of the wider objective of transforming Indochina from a battlefield into a marketplace.[14]

Regionally, Australia endeavored to play a constructive role in Southeast Asian multilateral diplomacy to enhance security dialogue, trust-building and practical cooperation—participating in both formal "track-one" and nonofficial "track-two" forums, seminars, and working groups. This was accompanied by the initiation of a multilayered process of physical security cooperation, which varied in depth from simple consultation to intelligence sharing, and the consolidation of joint defense exercises (such as those already undertaken

---

[13]In particular, regional multilateralism was viewed as an effective way of mitigating the threat of Chinese-U.S. conflict, which remained a palpable fear throughout the general Southeast Asian area.

[14]For further details see Evans and Grant, 1995, pp. 221–237; Frost, 1993; and Maley, 1993.

with Singapore and Malaysia through the Five Powers Defence Arrangements [FPDA]).[15]

Perhaps the most significant achievement was the signing of a mutual security treaty with Indonesia in 1995, the first such agreement that Australia had ever concluded with an Asian state and the first negotiated by Jakarta with any country (see Chapter Two) (Viviani, 1997, pp. 155–156; Dupont, 1996).

Added to this diplomatic program was an active socioeconomic and environmental agenda. Australia vigorously supported trade liberalization and integration throughout Southeast Asia, endorsing APEC as well as moves by ASEAN member states to establish a free trade area (to be known as the ASEAN Free Trade Area [AFTA]) by 2003.[16]

The government also took a leading role in advocating the need to focus resources and attention on regional ecological problems such as climate change, atmospheric pollution, sustainable development, biodiversity, and desertification.[17]

Finally, an assiduous effort was made to both strengthen and consolidate meaningful person-to-person links through the promotion of educational exchanges and tourism and by facilitating increased Asian immigration into the country.[18]

---

[15]The FPDA involved Australia, New Zealand, the UK, Singapore, and Malaysia. Operationally, the arrangements provide for joint military exercises and an integrated air defense system (IADS).

[16]At the Singapore Summit meeting of 1992, the (then) six member states of ASEAN agreed to establish an AFTA by the year 2010. In December 1995 this deadline was moved forward to 2003 (although given the relatively underdeveloped nature of their economies, Vietnam, Laos, and Myanmar—all now members of ASEAN—have been granted special dispensations to defer obligations under AFTA until 2006). AFTA is to be governed by a Common Effective Preferential Tariff (CEPT) scheme that covers about 90 percent of all products traded within ASEAN and provides for a 0–5 percent reduction of tariffs by the year 2003 or earlier. It was expected that about 88 percent of all products covered by the CEPT would already be at the 0–5 percent mark by 2000. The CEPT does not cover unprocessed agricultural commodities such as rice. It is hoped, however, that a small proportion of these products will be liberalized by the year 2010. (For further details see Leifer, 1996, pp. 45–46, and Menon, 1997, pp. 83–84.)

[17]For an overview of Australian environmental policies and initiatives between 1990 and 1995, see Harris, 1997, pp. 113–133, and Evans and Grant, 1995, pp. 162–169.

[18]See, for instance, Mackie, 1997, pp. 10–49, and Michele Langfield, 1997, pp. 28–56. Increased Asian migration was also very much a reaction to earlier racial barriers to entry (formalized in the White Australia Policy), which ran counter to the country's self-conceptualization as a tolerant liberal and multiethnic state. The White Policy originated with the Immigration Act of 1901, which was used to exclude certain (non-Western) migrants from entering Australia by requiring them to pass a written test in a language that they were not necessarily familiar with. This restrictive philosophy was especially emphasized following the outbreak of hostilities with Japan during World War II when Prime Minister John Curtin asserted that Australia "shall remain forever the home of the descendants of those people who came here in peace and order to establish in the South Seas an outpost of the British race." The Australian White Policy was gradually dismantled during the 1950s and 1960s, although it was not until 1973 that all barriers to immigration, on the basis of race, were removed.

In summing up these efforts, Viviani offered the following remarks:

> In the [1980s and] 1990s the Hawke Government embarked on an explicit strategy to enmesh Australia with Asia across [a wide] range of relations, to initiate a new regional security strategy. . . . By the end of 1995 the Keating Government could, and did, claim success on . . . these fronts. The country had shifted towards Asia, despite the backsliders, the cynics, the Europe [and U.S.]-first lobby and the anti-Asian migration lobby. . . . These were very substantial achievements given the history of the . . . long entrenched fears of Asia, and the cultural and family ties to [the West]. (Viviani, 1997, p. 168)

The John Howard Administration

In 1996, a new liberal-nationalist coalition led by John Howard, who was sworn in as Australia's prime minister in March of that year, replaced Keating's Labor government. Although Asian engagement was a main issue of the 1996 campaign, and despite Howard's own commitment to bring the United States alliance back to the center stage of Australian foreign policy, the overall direction of Canberra's external orientation has not changed substantially since 1996.

Southeast Asia is still viewed very much as a political priority as is the general need to enhance regional security cooperation and stability. In endorsing this stance, the current foreign minister, Alexander Downer, has specifically stated that "there is a national consensus on the importance of Australia's engagement with Asia and . . . a strong [understanding] that no side of Australian politics 'owns' the Asian vision." [19]

In line with this recognition of the need for regional engagement, Australia has continued to play a constructive role in both track-one and track-two multilateral diplomacy as well as moved to foster stable and mutually supportive bilateral government-government links. In 1997, several significant accords on information sharing were signed with Thailand, the Philippines, Vietnam, and China, doubling the number of Southeast Asian countries that regularly engage in security dialogues with Australia. That same year, an important maritime agreement was signed with Indonesia, which finally settled the frontiers between the two countries in the Arafura and Timor seas and eastern Indian Ocean.

Arguably of greater note was Canberra's response to the East Asian financial crisis, which first broke with the forced devaluation of the Thai baht in 1997. Between 1997 and 1998, several significant economic assistance and bailout packages were prepared, both unilaterally and in conjunction with the

---

[19] Alexander Downer, cited in Jones and Smith, 1999, pp. 452–453.

International Monetary Fund (IMF) (G. Smith, 1999, pp. 194–196). The purpose of these actions was, in the words of Alexander Downer, to emphasize the notion of "regional mateship" and to convey the message that Australia was not just a "fair-weather friend" but also "a genuinely close regional ally, in good times and in bad" (Downer, May 8, 1998).

If a difference does exist, it is in the conduct, rather than the substance, of foreign policy. In particular, the liberal-nationalist coalition has sought to pursue its objectives in a more pragmatic and less personal fashion than the former Labour administration had done. Regarding the Indonesian relationship, for instance, Howard was far less forceful in maintaining the strong personal ties that Keating had created with former Indonesian president Suharto (1967–1998), even if he did support the president to the very end.

In addition, there has been a greater acceptance by the current government of the continued salience of the United States alliance and a rejection of the idea that self-reliant defense, and the related focus on Southeast Asia, necessarily precludes the option of working in conjunction with Washington in regional and more-distant theaters. To this end, the Howard administration has conspicuously sought to balance the Keating emphasis on geography (which matters less in a globalized world) and Asia (whose own economic importance has been increasingly questioned since the 1997 financial crises) by developing and consolidating Australia's historical and strategic ties with America.[20]

As part of this approach, a concerted effort has been made to actively invest in high-end capabilities and the associated revolution in military affairs (RMA) to ensure full interoperability with United States defense assets. In addition, Howard has sought to position Australia as a natural bridge for raising and facilitating socioeconomic and political issues among Asia, Europe, and North America, a stance that became particularly evident during the IMF negotiations that followed Southeast Asia's 1997–1998 financial meltdown.

On the whole, however, engagement with Asia, and more specifically Southeast Asia, continues to form a basic objective of Australian foreign policy. As with Keating, Howard has recognized Indonesia as essential to this aim of regional engagement, not the least because of its size, geographic proximity, strategic influence, and preeminent position within ASEAN. Although the liberal-nationalist coalition has been prepared to adopt somewhat of a more forceful and less placatory line with Jakarta—a stance that became particularly clear in late 1998 to 1999 when the crisis in East Timor erupted—managing a stable bilateral partnership has always remained a key objective of the government.

---

[20]See, for instance, "Will Our Defense Dollars Be Enough?" 2000.

To better understand how Indonesia became such an integral component of Australian foreign policy and, consequently, why the present fallout in bilateral relations is viewed as being so serious, one needs to retrace the somewhat tumultuous history between the two countries over the past 50 years. That history is covered in Chapter Two.

Chapter Two

AUSTRALIA'S FOREIGN RELATIONS WITH INDONESIA: 1945 TO THE PRESENT

On a global scale, one would be hard pressed to find two nations as fundamentally distinct as Indonesia and Australia. Aside from the fact that both countries lie in the Asia-Pacific region and share a Melanesian contiguity, they share few things in common.

Indonesia, with a population of almost 220 million, is the world's fourth most populous country and its largest Muslim nation, occupying a 5,000-kilometer-long archipelago that consists of more than 17,000 islands and roughly 300 ethnic groups and languages. Australia, by contrast, is an overwhelmingly Western island-continent of 18 million people, whose federal commonwealth and democratic tradition and accompanying emphasis on individual rights contrast sharply with the unitary and (until at least recently) strongly authoritarian political culture of Indonesia (Evans and Grant, 1995, p. 198; Walters, 1997, pp. 157–158; "Downer Should Be a Realist," 2000).

This being said, Indonesia represents Australia's largest and, as a result, most important regional neighbor. More critically, its size and physical location have endowed it as one of the key players in organizations such as ASEAN and APEC. As such, it is a state that Canberra has little option but to deal with, all the more so as Australia tries to play a more active and meaningful role in the region. It was in this context that former prime minister Paul Keating declared in 1994: "No relationship offers greater potential, on the social, cultural or economic fronts, than this one with Indonesia. If we fail to get [it] right, and nurture and develop it, the whole web of [Australian regional] relations is incomplete" (*East Timor: Report of the Senate Foreign Affairs, Defence and Trade References Committee*, 1999, p. 871; "Fixed Relations," 1997).

This chapter examines the nature, scope, and dimension of evolving Australian foreign policy toward Indonesia. In many ways, the history of bilateral ties between the two countries over the past half-century has been akin to a roller coaster ride—one that has been conditioned by the dynamics of the Cold War and its aftermath as well as internal developments that have taken place in each of the two countries.

The period between 1945 and 1949 was cordial as Australia supported the Indonesian struggle for independence. The years between 1950 and 1965 were somewhat more strained and dominated both by the attitudes and predilections of the Sukarno government and the perceived imperatives of Cold War ideological politics. Relations began to improve with the emergence of Suharto's "New Order" government and the election of Australian Prime Minister Gough Whitlam, which saw Indonesia realign with the West and adopt a "regional good neighbor policy" and Australia (for the first time) explicitly emphasize an Asia-Pacific–oriented foreign policy.

In the late 1970s, Prime Minister Malcolm Fraser's return to the politics and rhetoric of the ideological predilections of the Cold War stymied further consolidation of bilateral relations, something that held true until the election of Keating who, with Foreign Minister Gareth Evans (1988 to 1996), orchestrated an external agenda that was heavily oriented toward Jakarta. A directed focus on Indonesia continued to underscore the John Howard administration and remained in place until the tumultuous events that engulfed East Timor in 1999 and 2000.

THE EARLY YEARS: 1945–1965

Australia's relationship with Indonesia began in earnest between 1945 and 1950 when Canberra played a significant role in supporting Jakarta's struggle for independence from the Netherlands. Australia was a natural advocate of the Indonesian cause due to its own history of British colonial rule and the bond that had been formed between the two countries as a result of the many troops that had served in Indonesia during World War II.

The government of Australian Prime Minister Benedict Chifley (1945–1949) ideologically supported the Indonesian nationalist revolutionary struggle against the Dutch and in 1947 represented the nation's interests in the United Nation's (UN) Good Offices Committee, arguing for international recognition of an independent Indonesian state. In 1950, Canberra cosponsored Jakarta's official admission to the UN, appointing its first Ambassador to the Republic that same year (Evans and Grant, 1995, p. 188; Walters, 1997, pp. 160–161). According to Margaret George, a well-respected historian of the period, by 1950 Australia had emerged as the "most prominent diplomatic protagonist of the Indonesian government," a factor that helped to engender considerable good will between the two countries (George, 1980, p. 167).

During the 1950s and 1960s, however, bilateral relations underwent a substantial cooling off as a result of three main factors, all of which brought their own agendas and sets of problems: Cold War ideological politics, decolonization in West Irian, and national reconstruction in Malaysia.

The onset of the global bilateral struggle between the United States and the former Soviet Union undoubtedly had a major impact on Australian-Indonesian relations. The key political figure in Jakarta at this time was President Sukarno, an outspoken leader of nonalignment and anticolonialism who adopted an increasingly explicitly pro-China stance as part of a wider rhetorical campaign against great power domination. Coming at a time when the Indonesian Communist Party (PKI) was rapidly growing in influence and set against the seemingly inexorable rise of revolutionary left-wing activism and insurgency in the Asia-Pacific, concerns emerged in Canberra that a threatening quasi-Communist state was being established to its immediate north.

These developments served to gradually freeze the warmth of the immediate postwar relationship to such an extent that by 1963 the government of Robert Menzies was specifically identifying Indonesia as posing the main strategic threat to Australia and its territories (Walters, 1997, pp. 162–163; McDougall, 1998, p. 202). Against this general background arose the decolonization of West Irian and national reconstruction in Malaysia, two issues that came to dominate the Australian-Indonesian relationship during the 1950s and early 1960s.

The issue of West Irian, formerly known as West or Dutch New Guinea (and today as Irian Jaya or West Papua), was left unresolved at the time of Indonesian independence, with the territory left out of the 1949 Charter of Transfer of Sovereignty that conferred statehood to Jakarta (McDougall, 1998, p. 203). The main justification for the exclusion was that, as Melanesians, the indigenous peoples of West Irian were ethnically distinct from Indonesians and should therefore be governed separately. Sukarno had always been vigorously opposed to this decision and as his anti-imperialist rhetoric gathered pace during the 1950s, his determination to oust the Dutch from one of their last colonial outposts also grew (Walters, 1997, p. 162).

Menzies came out strongly against the transfer of West Irian to Indonesian sovereignty, largely because it was feared that any moves in that direction would prompt Jakarta to make claims on the Australian-administered eastern half of the island, threatening a key link in Canberra's northern line of defense. The fact that Sukarno was adopting an increasingly radical, pro-Communist stance certainly did nothing to alleviate these concerns.[1] The Australian attitude

---

[1] See, for instance, Millar, 1978, p. 227.

instilled a significant degree of resentment in Indonesia, polluting the bilateral relationship for more than a decade.

Ultimately, however, Canberra was forced to back down over the West Irian issue, with neither the United States nor the United Kingdom prepared to support its position and risk antagonizing Jakarta further over what was regarded as a "worthless piece of land and a dubious application of principle" (Mackie, 1963, p. 273). In 1963, a settlement was finally reached in which the Dutch, under strong pressure from Washington, agreed to transfer West Irian to Indonesian sovereignty after a short period of UN administration (McDougall, 1998, p. 203). As Patrick Walters notes, "Australia had no choice but to meekly acquiesce" (Walters, 1997, p. 162).

Buoyed by its victory in West Irian, Jakarta was eager to campaign against the newly formed Malaysian Federation,[2] which Sukarno viewed as a neocolonial edifice that was designed to perpetrate British influence in Southeast Asia and extend the power of the conservative Malayan state. In January 1963, the Indonesian President declared the initiation of a policy of "confrontation" (*konfrontasi*) against Malaysia, which combined diplomatic overtures to garner support (or at least neutrality) from the Afro-Asian community with low-level armed incursions into different parts of the Federation (particularly Borneo) (McDougall, 1998, p. 204).

Konfrontasi marked the nadir of Australian-Indonesian relations in addition to severely straining Jakarta's diplomatic standing with both the United States and the United Kingdom. Not only did the campaign coincide with the resolution of the West Irian dispute (which had been settled counter to Australia's interests), it also came hot on the heels of the Cuban Missile Crisis (October 16–28, 1962), which had brought the world to the brink of nuclear disaster. The Menzies government, already suspicious about the emergence of a Jakarta-Beijing axis, grew progressively more anxious as Sukarno's erratic and increasingly authoritarian stewardship fostered instability in the heart of Southeast Asia—a concern shared by both London and Washington (Walters, 1997, p. 163).

Although a concerted attempt was made to stabilize the situation—even as Australian, British, and Indonesian troops faced one another in the jungles of Borneo—Canberra was determined to prevent Jakarta from assuming the upper hand. Indeed, the Australian government made it clear that it was prepared to use force in Malaysia if necessary: "It may, of course, emerge that seeking friendship on the one hand and pursuing an inflexible determination to defend

---

[2] The Malaysian Federation was composed of Malaya, Singapore, and the Borneo territories of Sabah and Sarawak; Singapore left the Federation in 1965, largely as a result of ethnic Chinese politics.

what and whom we believe to be right may on occasions prove incompatible. If they do, the latter must prevail and we shall find ourselves set on a collision course" (Barwick, 1964). Unlike the situation in Irian Jaya, Canberra had the support of the United States and United Kingdom, something that gave the threat added credence.

Ironically it was a domestic event in Indonesia that helped to prevent a major clash from occurring between Canberra and Jakarta. After three years of confrontation and with inflation, foreign debt, unemployment, and poverty all spiraling out of control, a coup was attempted by a group of disaffected leftist army officers in September 1965.[3] The attempted seizure of power was quelled within 24 hours by the army's strategic reserve force (KOSTRAD), which used the incident as a pretext for asserting its own power. This effectively marked the demise of the Sukarno era and paved the way for the establishment of the New Order government under General Suharto, the commander-in-chief of KOSTRAD (Walters, 1997, p. 163; McDougall, 1998, p. 204).

THE NEW ORDER PERIOD: 1965–1988

The emergence of the New Order government marked a watershed in Australian-Indonesian relations. Suharto quickly embarked on a "regional good neighbor policy" to correct the poor international image Jakarta had fostered in the twilight years of Sukarno's rule. The new president also played an instrumental role in the formation of ASEAN, investing considerable diplomatic capital in the new regional body (Walters, 1997, p. 164). These initiatives helped to offset Australian concerns about a destabilizing Indonesian agenda, providing the basis for a rapprochement between the two countries.

Matters were further availed by the severe nature of the Indonesian economic plight, which by 1965 had reached unprecedented proportions (per capita income at this time was only $190 in U.S. dollars) (McDougall, 1998, p. 206; Hill, 1994, p. 57). Suharto quickly turned to Australia (and the West in general) for economic assistance, which Canberra was keen to grant as a way of promoting recovery and, thereby, boosting political stability. By 1970, overall aid stood at $15 million Australian (compared with an average of only $1 million Australian per annum while Sukarno was in power)—a sum that was superseded only by the financial assistance to Papua New Guinea. Australia also emerged as a leading participant in the Inter-Governmental Group on Indonesia (IGGI), a multilateral assistance consortium composed of Western countries that was

---

[3]It was widely portrayed throughout Indonesia that the coup was instigated at the behest of the PKI, which fed into a mass killing spree of Communists and their suspected sympathizers. The subsequent death toll is generally agreed to have been between 200,000 and 250,000. (See McDougall, 1998, p. 204, and Legge, 1984, pp. 398–399.)

instituted to facilitate economic recovery in the archipelagic state (Millar, 1978, p. 234; Walters, 1997, p. 164).

A highly useful facet of these economic ties was that they formed a favorable basis from which to consolidate relations in other areas. Personal contacts between government officials from both countries increased and the beginnings of meaningful defense cooperation, in the form of officer exchanges and the sharing of intelligence, began to occur (Catley and Dugis, 1998, p. 151). The government of Gough Whitlam that succeeded Menzies in 1972 kept the momentum going, boosting the level of economic and military aid provided to Jakarta as part of the overall objective of further developing Australia's involvement in, and engagement with, Asia (Walters, 1997, p. 164).

It was into this political environment that the East Timor issue erupted in 1975. In the weeks preceding Jakarta's invasion of the territory, Whitlam had (secretly) intimated that Australia would not actively oppose a peaceful Indonesian takeover of the territory providing due regard was paid to the aspirations of the local population (Monk, 2000a; Indonesian security analysts, 2000). The violent nature of the subsequent invasion, however, generated widespread animosity throughout Australia, where a strong emotional attachment was felt toward the East Timor people (see Chapter Three). Indeed, the annexation of East Timor by Indonesia proved to be a key factor in undermining initial bilateral relations with the new Liberal coalition of Malcolm Fraser that had replaced Whitlam's Labor government in the fall of 1975.[4]

Nonetheless, in what was to become a characteristic feature of central government policy throughout the 1980s and most of the 1990s, Canberra moved to quickly acknowledge the inevitability of Jakarta's annexation for the sake of ensuring wider economic and political interests. As Chapter Three notes, much of this accommodationist stance was initially oriented toward accessing offshore resources in the Timor Gap; however, the policy progressively came to be defined more in the context of Australia's wider Southeast Asian engagement efforts.

In 1976, de facto recognition was accorded to Indonesia's incorporation of East Timor, with full *de jure* endorsement granted three years later (Evans and Grant, 1995, p. 200; Walters, 1997, p. 165; McDougall, 1998, p. 215). It should be noted that no other country has accorded a similar act of legal recognition to Jakarta's annexation of the province.

---

[4]On assuming power, Fraser backed a UN resolution calling for East Timorese self-determination, which particularly provoked the ire of Jakarta. In addition, he introduced a new protectionist trade policy, which targeted a number of manufactured products from Indonesia that, hitherto, had enjoyed steady export growth.

Although a potentially serious rift was thus avoided over the East Timor issue, Fraser's Cold War rhetoric directed against the Soviet Union, particularly after Moscow's invasion of Afghanistan in 1979, and his renewed emphasis on the United States alliance contrasted with Indonesia's continued reservations about great power influence within Southeast Asia. These differing perspectives, which also largely underscored the subsequent administration of Australian Prime Minister Bob Hawke, limited the further maturation of the Australian-Indonesian relationship and placed a ceiling on the extent to which Australia was able to play a more constructive role in the affairs of Southeast Asia during most of the 1980s.

1988 TO THE PRESENT

In March 1986, a major review of Australia's defense capabilities was under-taken by Canberra. Known as the Dibb report (after the document's author, Paul Dibb, a leading academic and strategic analyst in Australia), this assessment provided for a more independent policy of self-reliance, a posture that was subsequently embodied in the Hawke government's Defence White Paper of 1987. The Dibb review provided a frank assessment of Australia's strategic geography, arguing, at least in defense terms, that Indonesia remained Canberra's most important regional neighbor. It also pointed to Australia's fundamental security interest in promoting stability in Southeast Asia, free from interference by potentially hostile external powers (Walters, 1997, p. 166).

Foreign Minister Gareth Evans portrayed the White Paper as a "conceptual watershed" in Australian external relations, arguing that it allowed for the institution of a more independent, liberated, and regionally focused defense posture (Evans and Grant, 1995, p. 29). Evans set about adapting Canberra's grand strategy around a new nucleus specifically geared toward the Asia-Pacific, embarking on a set of policies that later came to be known as "comprehensive engagement" (see Chapter One). The main foundational structure of this reorientation resided in the Australian-Indonesian relationship, the overall significance of which began to take on added significance in Canberra. Together with Ali Alatas, Jakarta's newly appointed foreign minister, Evans sought to place official contacts on a new footing.

The first move in this direction was the establishment of Australia-Indonesia Institute (AII) in 1988, which provided funds to promote person-to-person con-tacts through a host of academic, cultural, and educational exchanges. In 1989, Evans and Alatas promulgated the *New Framework for the Australia-Indonesia Relationship*, which called for more frequent consulting and monitoring of re-lations between the two countries. That same year, the landmark Timor Gap Zone of Cooperation Treaty (TGZCT) was successfully negotiated, allowing shared access to potentially rich oil and gas deposits in the Timor Sea as well as joint responsibility for matters such as maritime surveillance, environmental protection, and customs and immigration procedures (Walters, 1997, p. 169).

Hawke's continuing emphasis on the U.S. alliance, however, served to artificially constrain the full development of Evans's regional agenda. Matters were further complicated by the prime minister's forceful condemnation of the Dili Massacre (November 11, 1991), where Indonesian troops used live ammunition to disperse supporters of Fretilin (an East Timorese pro-indendence party) who had marched to the capital's Santa Cruz cemetery to join mourners who were burying a pro-independence youth killed the previous day. The number of casualties has never been confirmed, but it is known that more than 200 were either killed or wounded. The incident marked the beginning of the inexorable process of international criticism and internal East Timorese opposition that led to the August 1999 popular consultation and the territory's eventual independence.

Managing the relationship with Indonesia undoubtedly emerged as one of the key facets of Australian foreign policy between 1991 and 1995, with Keating seeing it as essential to the success of Canberra's wider Southeast Asian engagement efforts. Shortly after taking over from Hawke, the new prime minister chose to make the Indonesian Republic his first official overseas port of call. During the trip to Jakarta in April 1992, Keating, who was careful not to bring up the issue of the Dili Massacre, established an informal but highly important alliance with Suharto that was to have a decisive bearing on future bilateral ties. As Walters observes,

> The success of Keating's initial visit and the [rapport] he forged with Soeharto gave new impetus to official relations. In the eyes of many Indonesian observers, the Keating-Soeharto alliance . . . had a vital bearing on how both Indonesian officialdom and business interests [perceived] Australia. From the perspective of Australian business, doors that had been closed before April 1992 were suddenly opening up across the archipelago (Walters, 1997, p. 172).

Between April 1992 and December 1995, Keating made no less than six additional visits to the Republic, during which time a dedicated Australia-Indonesia Ministerial Forum (AIMF) was established. Meeting every two years, the AIMF was an extremely important initiative, providing an institutional framework for the further development of official bilateral ties across a highly diverse range of issues.[5] By the mid-1990s, these agreements were producing an intense level of cooperative activity in sectors as diverse as health, the environment, education

---

[5]It should be noted that this orientation fit well with Suharto, who wanted "ballast to the south" and who was keen to formalize a divergent policy agenda with Australia as part of Indonesia's regional competition with Malaysia.

and training, and science and technology (Evans and Grant, 1995, pp. 202–203; Walters, 1997, p. 173).

The apex of Keating's overtures to Jakarta, however, came with the signing of the unprecedented Australia-Indonesia AMS in December 1995. The three main articles of the accord are worth quoting in full:

- Article 1: The Parties undertake to consult at ministerial level on a regular basis about matters affecting their common security and to develop such cooperation as would benefit their own security and that of the region.

- Article 2: The Parties undertake to consult each other in the case of adverse challenges to either party or to their common security interests and, if appropriate, to consider measures which might be taken either individually or jointly and in accordance with the processes of each Party.

- Article 3: The Parties agree to promote—in accordance with the policies and priorities of each—mutually beneficial cooperative activities in the security field to be identified by the two Parties (Lowry, 1996, pp. 31–32).

Although not a full-fledged treaty in the sense of imposing formal defense commitments, the AMS nevertheless represented an extremely significant development. Not only did the accord lend further credibility to Australia's desire to constructively engage with its Southeast Asian neighbors, it was also highly important in a symbolic sense. For Canberra, this stemmed from the fact that the agreement was reached with a country that its own troops had directly faced during the Malaysian "confrontation." Just as important, for Indonesia the AMS was the first security agreement that the country had concluded with any polity, Asian or otherwise. The major implication for Canberra was that the accord gave the country new and powerful credentials as a state of Southeast Asia, something that had long been denied by other influential regional actors such as Malaysia, which had repeatedly portrayed Australia as a distinctly Western state (Smith, Cox, and Burchill, 1997, p. 155; Viviani, 1997, p. 156; Brown, Frost, and Sherlock, 1996; Dupont, 1996, pp. 49–62; "How the PM Has Been Working Overtime to Forge Asian Link," 1995).

A directed focus on Jakarta was equally characteristic of John Howard's subsequent approach to regional engagement (at least until late 1998). Perhaps the most visible indication of this was the government's 1997 Foreign Policy White Paper, which specifically identified Indonesia as one of the country's most substantial regional interests. Reflecting these sentiments, Howard quickly secured an important Maritime Delimitation Treaty, which settled all frontiers between the two countries in the Arafura Sea ("Fixed Relations," 1997). This treaty was then followed by a period of intense diplomatic activity aimed at lobbying the IMF to relax the conditions attached to the Indonesian restructuring loans at the height of the East Asian financial crisis (G. Smith,

1999, pp. 194–195; "We're Solid in a Crisis," 1998). Rationalizing the policy during an address to the Australian-American Association in New York, Howard's foreign minister, Alexander Downer, made the point that "being seen through the IMF to bully and cajole [Jakarta] into a particular political paradigm will [merely] . . . invite a negative and lasting backlash from Indonesians [to the complete detriment of our regional engagement effort]" (Downer, June 8, 1998).

In sum, one of the most important bases of Australia's post–Cold War foreign policy has been to foster links with Indonesia as part of the wider endeavor to comprehensively integrate with Southeast Asia. To this end, vigorous overtures have been made to establish and cement aid, investment, security, and political ties with Jakarta, while moving to avoid any potential pitfalls that could undermine the bilateral partnership.

Nowhere has this been more apparent than with East Timor, which for more than 20 years Canberra assiduously avoided unnecessarily highlighting for the sake of maintaining a wider bilateral relationship with Jakarta. As noted earlier in this chapter, the most visible expression of this policy was the *de jure* recognition of East Timor's annexation by Indonesia, a legal act of endorsement that was not matched by any other Western state and which was upheld by successive governments throughout the 1980s and most of the 1990s.

In 1999, however, events in East Timor took on an unprecedented dynamic, provoking a crisis that has had an impact not only on the future course of Australian defense and foreign policy, but which has also completely altered the nature and scope of the country's relations with Indonesia. In Chapter Three, I turn to an examination of these issues.

Chapter Three

THE EAST TIMOR ISSUE AND ITS IMPACT ON AUSTRALIAN-INDONESIAN RELATIONS

East Timor has been a perennial problem complicating the bilateral Australian-Indonesian relationship for more than 25 years. Although Canberra is the only Western government to have formally acknowledged Jakarta's claim to sovereignty over the territory—granting *de jure* recognition in 1979—the topic has been passionately debated within Australia.

Historically, there is great emotional attachment to East Timor as a result of the World War II experience and the critical role that the island's populace played in supporting Australian (and Dutch) guerrilla operations against occupying Japanese forces. This assistance, which led to the deaths of some 40,000 local civilians, has evolved into near folklore status among certain segments of the Australian community and has certainly helped to instill a sense of public debt that is felt to be owed to the East Timorese people (Dunn, 1983, pp. 22–26; Salla, 1995, p. 207; Cotton, 2000a, pp. 1–2).

There has also been an active and ongoing media interest in the Indonesian annexation. Initially, much of this interest stemmed from the killing of five Australian newsmen in Balibo in East Timor on the eve of Jakarta's invasion. Many journalists have claimed that the murders were directly carried out by Indonesian commandos during a covert mission (*Operasi Flamboyant*) to capture key towns in the East/West Timor border regions (Ball and McDonald, 2000, p. 30; *East Timor: Report of the Senate Foreign Affairs, Defence and Trade References Committee*, 1999, p. 133; Cotton, 2000a, p. 3).[1] The media's focus on the situation has since been sustained by the increasingly questionable human rights record of the Indonesian military in the province, their racially biased attitudes toward the eastern Melanesian peoples, and the army's documented

---

[1]Australian journalists have repeatedly claimed that Prime Minister Gough Whitlam had direct knowledge of the killings but chose to suppress the incident for the sake of preserving relations with Jakarta.

involvement in large-scale atrocities such as the Dili Massacre (discussed later in this chapter).

The sizable East Timorese refugee community in Australia, which currently numbers around 20,000, has further complicated the situation. These displaced people have helped to highlight the issue of Jakarta's annexation of the territory as a crucial test case for Canberra's commitment to, and emphasis on, liberal democracy and basic humanitarian standards.[2] In so doing, they have also been instrumental in mobilizing and politicizing several public interest and lobbying groups, providing a domestic context that no Australian government has been able to ignore (Monk, 2000b, and Barton, 2000).

However, for the most part, the cause of East Timorese self-determination (and, arguably human rights) has been sacrificed for the sake of maintaining the wider strategic partnership with Indonesia, which is itself seen as critical to the success of the general push into Southeast Asia (Cotton, 2000a, p. 2; McDougall, 1998, p. 212). It was only in the latter part of the 1990s that a change began to occur in this policy, culminating with the dispatch of Australian troops in September 1999 to lead an armed multinational UN intervention peacekeeping team mandated to forcibly restore order in East Timor.

OVERVIEW OF THE EAST TIMOR CONFLICT

East Timor occupies half of the island of Timor, which lies along the southern rim of the Indonesian archipelago, just 300 miles to the north of the port city of Darwin, Australia. The territory covers an area of 14,874 square kilometers and in 1999 had a registered voter population of 450,000 (Singh, 1996, p. 1320; *Indonesia 1996: An Official Handbook,* 1996; "E. Timor Rivals Plan for War, Peace," 1999).[3] The eastern part of Timor was settled and colonized by Portuguese Catholic missionaries during the sixteenth century, with the western half falling under Dutch military control in 1656. Following World War II, West Timor was incorporated into the Indonesian nation along with the rest of the Dutch East Indies; East Timor, however, remained a colony of Portugal (Aditjondro, 1994, p. 7; Schwarz, 1994, pp. 198–199; Hastings, 2000, pp. 59–63).

---

[2]During the post–Cold War period, Australia has consistently defined its overall foreign policy orientation as consistent with the norms and assumptions of good international citizenship (GIC). This asserts an aspiration toward the development of a new type of international order in which state behavior is regulated and contained within a system of common rules and universally upheld and transnational values. Above all, GIC affirms the need to implement and abide by such global activities as international law, human rights, and justice. (For further details see Evans and Grant, 1995, pp. 8–12; Goldsworthy, 1995, pp. 171–189; and Stokes, 1996, pp. 1–10.)

[3]For a detailed summary of East Timor's main economic and social development indicators, see *East Timor: Report of the Senate Foreign Affairs, Defence and Trade References Committee,* 1999, pp. 7–33.

The decisive moment for East Timorese nationalism occurred not in Southeast Asia but in Europe. Since the 1920s, a succession of authoritarian right-wing governments had ruled Portugal, involving the country in various anticolonial conflicts, including wars in Mozambique, Angola, and Guinea Bissau. Increasingly politicized by these experiences and recognizing that Lisbon no longer had the economic capacity to maintain an overseas empire, the military began to take on a progressively rebellious and overtly leftist stance. Coalescing around a so-called Armed Forces Movement (MFA), these fractious elements staged a coup in 1974, successfully overthrowing the dictatorship of Portuguese Prime Minister Marcello Caetano (1968–1974). The new government immediately endorsed support for decolonization, announcing its intention to grant independence to all overseas Portuguese territories, including East Timor, as soon as possible (McDougall, 1998, p. 213; Whitlam, 2000, p. 140).

Within a few weeks, a handful of political parties had formed within East Timor to contest independence elections, which had been tentatively scheduled for 1975. Three front-runners quickly emerged:

- The Timorese Democratic Union (UDT)—Founded by Mario Carrascalao, Francisco Lopez da Cruz, and Domingos d'Oliveria, the party called for three things: self-determination for the East Timorese people, an intermediate stage of political autonomy before the attainment of full independence, and the eventual establishment of a federation with Portugal.

- The Timorese Social Democratic Association, subsequently renamed the Revolutionary Front for an Independent East Timor (Fretilin)—Like the UDT, Fretilin was also pro-independence. However, the party advocated the immediate attainment of self-rule and was far more socialistic in outlook, retaining close links to left-wing nationalist groups in both Portugal and Africa.[4] The party stressed the need for literacy programs, agricultural development, and the reassurance of a unique Timorese culture.

- The Association for the Integration of Timor into Indonesia (Apodeti)—The least popular of the three main parties, Apodeti called for the autonomous integration of East Timor into the Republic of East Timor in accordance with international law (Aditjondro, 1994, p. 8; Hastings, 2000, pp. 65–67; McDougall, 1998, p. 214).

---

[4]The acronym *Fretilin*, for instance, bore a strong resemblance to *Frelimo*, the name of the left-wing nationalist group that had fought against Portuguese colonial rule in Mozambique.

At this stage, the Indonesian government officially dismissed all interest in East Timor, with the foreign minister publicly stating that Jakarta would fully support the outcome of the electoral process and would strive to maintain friendly relations for the benefit of both countries. Growing popular support for Fretilin and its leftist nationalist agenda, however, led to a gradual reorientation in Jakarta, with the army, in particular, expressing concern about possibly having to share a common border with a radical Communist state at the margin of a fissiparous archipelago (*East Timor: Report of the Senate Foreign Affairs, Defence and Trade References Committee*, 1999, pp. 130–133; Leifer, 1996, p. 254).

In the face of growing Indonesian hostility and increasingly overt support for Apodeti, the two main independence parties—UDT and Fretilin—banded together in early 1975, announcing an unequivocal platform of total independence, rejection of integration, and repudiation of colonialism to be tested in popular elections by November 1976 (Schwarz, 1994, pp. 201–202).

The coalition, however, was short-lived due to mistrust and suspicion on both sides: Fretilin doubted the UDT's commitment to total independence while UDT conservatives, especially landowners, were uncomfortable with Fretilin's increasingly radical socialist rhetoric. Playing on these internal divisions, officials in Jakarta were able to convince a number of key UDT members of the virtues of integration, leading to a U-turn in the party's policy and its subsequent (Indonesian-backed) alliance with Apodeti in mid-1975.

Increasing tension in the months that followed culminated with a Fretilin announcement of armed insurrection against all "traitors of the fatherland." Drawing on its considerable support in the countryside and exploiting the general unwillingness of the Portuguese government to commit troops to the increasingly restive province, the Revolutionary Front quickly overran the joint UDT-Apodeti forces gaining control of virtually all East Timor by September 1975 (Dunn, 2000, pp. 76–80; Schwarz, 1994, pp. 201–202).

By now, Indonesia was prepared to throw its full weight behind what it called the anti-Communist UDT-Apodeti alliance, sanctioning the use of covert commando teams to help keep pressure on independence forces. Fearing that a major military intervention was imminent, Fretilin proclaimed the creation of the Democratic Republic of East Timor on November 28, 1975. Nine days later on December 7, justifying his decision on the grounds that he wished to ensure that the majority's wish to integrate with the Republic of Indonesia should prevail, Indonesian President Suharto ordered a full-scale sea and airborne invasion of East Timor.

The taking of the territory was a violent affair with heavy casualties reported on both sides and in the civilian population. In response to this growing humanitarian crisis, the UN issued a number of declarations condemning the

Indonesian invasion and demanding an immediate and full troop withdrawal. Jakarta ignored the statements and on December 17 announced a provisional government in Dili headed by an Apodeti official and the UDT's Lopez da Cruz. The following May, the interim administration convened a People's Assembly in which 37 hand-picked delegates voted for integration with Indonesia. Arguing that this vote constituted a "free and willing act of Timorese self-determination," Suharto declared East Timor to be Indonesia's twenty-seventh province on July 17, 1976 (McDougall, 1998, p. 251; Singh, 1996, p. 1322; Schwarz, 1994, p. 204; Whitlam, 2000, pp. 143–146).

The 1975 annexation of East Timor sparked a major Fretilin insurgency, which by the time of the August 1999 popular consultation had cost the Indonesian armed forces several thousand lives and created an average annual military bill of at least $2.25 million (Australian) (Defense officials, December 15, 2000). The response initiated by Jakarta was as absolute as it was severe, involving a litany of basic human rights violations that ranged from arbitrary arrests and beatings to torture, summary executions, and, at times, mass murder.[5]

A watershed in the scale of this brutality was reached in November 1991 when Indonesian forces indiscriminately fired into a protest march that had been instituted to mourn the death of a pro-independence activist in Dili, killing and wounding hundreds of civilians.[6] The presence of seven international journalists at the scene of the massacre ensured that details of the shootings were quickly transmitted around the world, highlighting for the first time the nature and extent of Jakarta's intervention in East Timor (Henderson, 1999/2000, p. 66; *East Timor: Report of the Senate Foreign Affairs, Defence and Trade References Committee*, 1999, pp. 86-87).[7] One eyewitness to the shootings, Russell Anderson, gave the following account of the events surrounding the 1991 tragedy:

> Bob Muntz and I decided we should leave. I had taken ten hurried steps north along the cemetery wall and was glancing back to see the helmets of the military front line bobbing up and down, jogging or marching towards the crowd. The crowd began to walk backwards, walk away [and] some were already running. Suddenly a few shots rang out continued by an explosive volley of automatic rifle fire that persisted for 2 to 3 minutes. It sounded like the whole fifteen in the front row had their fingers pressed firmly on the trigger. They were firing directly into the crowd. I ran like everybody else. . . . Most people, especially in

---

[5]For an overview of human rights violations committed in East Timor between 1975 and 1999 see *East Timor: Report of the Senate Foreign Affairs, Defence and Trade References Committee*, 1999, pp. 82–90.

[6]The official Indonesian figure is 50 dead and 91 injured.

[7]For two good overviews of the Dili Massacre see Schwarz, 1994, pp. 211–222, and Aditjondro, 1994, pp. 11–20.

that initial burst of fire would have been shot in the back running away. ... In my opinion it was a cold blooded butcherous massacre. Statements about orders like "don't fire" being mistaken for "fire" do not ring true. The firing went on and on. The foreigners who were not brandishing or throwing anything received the same treatment as the East Timorese. The only difference was the foreigners, those still alive, were able to flee the country and tell what happened."[8]

Overall, the military occupation is thought to have cost the lives of at least 50,000 East Timorese, although certain commentators have put the total at between two and six times this figure (Aditjondro, 1994, pp. 37–39; Chomsky, 1978; Cotton, 1999, p. 237; *East Timor: Report of the Senate Foreign Affairs, Defence and Trade References Committee*, 1999, pp. 79–82; Firth, 1999, p. 192; Schwarz, 1994, pp. 205–206; "The East Timor Crisis," 1999, p. 1). If the higher estimate is true (the true human toll has never been established), on a proportionate basis it would be comparable in scale with the number of fatalities that occurred in Cambodia under the Pol Pot regime (Cotton, 1999, p. 237).

As long as Suharto remained in place as the undisputed leader of Indonesia, there was little prospect of a change occurring in the status of East Timor. Indeed throughout the entire period of his tenure as president, policy with regard to the territory rested on three nonnegotiable principles: First, the majority of East Timorese wished to be recognized as loyal Indonesians; second, the province's integration into the Republic had been validated by a legitimate act of self-determination in 1976; and third, the matter was therefore a closed issue that did not have to be re-opened (Schwarz, 1994, pp. 227–228).

Suharto also framed the debate of East Timorese self-determination in the wider context of maintaining the territorial integrity of the Indonesian state. More specifically, he consistently warned that any move to accede to the province's independence demands would inevitably galvanize secessionist pressures elsewhere on the archipelago to the detriment of national, regional, and possibly even international stability (Indonesian security analysts, 2000).

It was only following Suharto's May 1998 resignation in favor of his civilian vice president, B. J. Habibie, that real change in East Timor became a distinct possibility.[9] Announcing his intention to move Indonesia toward a true pluralist democratic system, Habibie committed himself to finding a genuine settlement to the East Timor conflict as quickly as possible. An ensuing round of national

---

[8]Russell Anderson, cited in *East Timor: Report of the Senate Foreign Affairs, Defence and Trade References Committee*, 1999, p. 86.

[9]Suharto's resignation was itself forced by spiraling civilian unrest in Java, growing national financial turmoil, and increasing international pressure for regional self-determination.

and international shuttle diplomacy conducted through his foreign minister, Ali Alatas, culminated with the landmark and completely unexpected decision in January 1999 to let the East Timorese decide for themselves whether they wished to remain in Indonesia or choose the alternate path of statehood (Cotton, 2000b, pp. 4–5; Downer, 2000, p. 5; "It's Time for Timor," 1999). [10]

In negotiating a comprehensive agreement with Portugal (which continued to assert its legal sovereignty over the territory) on May 5, 1999, Indonesia conceded to allow an internationally administered secret ballot to take place in East Timor in which the people would be asked to approve or reject a regional autonomy package offered by Jakarta. A "popular consultation" (at Indonesia's insistence the negotiations assiduously avoided using the terms "vote" or "referendum") overseen by an international monitoring force, the UN Assistance Mission in East Timor (UNAMET), [11] was subsequently held on August 30, 1999. Despite a concerted policy of intimidation by pro-integrationist militias, many of whom had been armed and trained by elements within the security forces, [12] this returned an overwhelming vote (78.5 percent) against the autonomy proposal, thus in effect endorsing independence. [13]

As soon as the results of the poll were announced, a surge of civil violence erupted across East Timor. Principally instigated by the pro-integrationist militias and either actively or passively supported by the armed forces, [14] this highly destructive campaign was primarily aimed at revenge, although it was also designed to serve as a warning to other Indonesian-controlled territories of what they could expect if they pressed for independence. In the weeks that followed, so-called *Operasi Sapu Jagad* (Operation Clean Sweep) led to the execu-

---

[10] Although this decision and U-turn in policy was framed in the context of democratization, most commentators feel that it had more to do with President Habibie's general unpredictability as well as his confidence that any consultation (that is, a referendum) on East Timor's future would return a vote in favor of remaining part of Indonesia (Defense officials, October 16, 2000).

[11] The role of UNAMET in the period leading up to the popular consultation was limited to advising the Indonesian police during the operational phase of the August 30, 1999, vote and supervising the escort of ballot boxes to and from the polling stations. (McFarlane and Maley, 2001, p. 13.) For a detailed discussion of the May 5 agreements providing for the dispatch of UNAMET see Maley, 2001, pp. 63–71, 70–72.

[12] The security forces were completely opposed to any question of granting independence to East Timor, especially given the number of casualties they had suffered trying to keep the territory an integral part of Indonesia. Almost immediately, elements within the military and Kopassus Special Forces set about training and arming pro-integrationist militias (sections of which had already been used against Fretilin as part of an unseen ABRI [Angkatan Bersenjata Republik Indonesia, which translates to "the Armed Forces of Indonesia"] "third force") to put pressure on the independence movement, sabotage the vote, and thereby guarantee the "right result" (McFarlane, 2000; Cotton, 2000b, p. 10).

[13] See, for instance, Henderson, 1999/2000, p. 67, and "The East Timor Crisis," 1999, p. 1.

[14] When the results of the referendum were returned, ABRI was shattered, taking out both its anger and frustration by giving free rein to the pro-integrationist militias to initiate a bloody campaign of reprisals against those who had voted for independence.

tions and slaughter of some 3,000 to 4,000 East Timorese, the displacement of hundreds of thousands of civilians from their homes, widespread attacks against UN personnel and equipment,[15] and the destruction of as much as 70 percent of the territory's physical infrastructure (Chopra 2000, p. 27; McFarlane and Maley, 2001, p. 30; *East Timor: Report of the Senate Foreign Affairs, Defence and Trade References Committee*, 1999, pp. 92–95; "Thousands Flee Homes in E. Timor," 1999; "E. Timor Rivals Plan for War, Peace," 1999; "Violence-Torn E. Timor Put Under Martial Law," 1999).[16]

Intense international pressure and criticism over Habibie's inability to control the rapidly deteriorating situation eventually forced him to consent to an Indonesian withdrawal from East Timor and deployment of an Australian-led UN peacekeeping force as a prelude to independence ("The East Timor Crisis," 1999, p. 1; "Indonesia Asks for UN Force to Calm E. Timor," 1999; "UN Plans for E. Timor Authority," 1999). With the subsequent arrival of the 9,000-strong INTERFET force on September 20, 1999, and ensuing establishment of a UN Transitional Authority in East Timor (UNTAET)[17] a month later, Jakarta's 25-year-long attempt to integrate the province effectively came to an end.[18]

---

[15]UNAMET, for instance, was equipped with 280 four-wheel-drive Land Rovers when it was deployed to East Timor. Between the August consultation and subsequent arrival of INTERFET, about half of these vehicles were completely destroyed or stolen, with many of the remaining heavily vandalized.

[16]The most notorious militia was the Aitarak (Thorn) Gang. Led by Eurico Guterres, the group was reportedly responsible for some of the worst carnage in Dili in the immediate aftermath of the August 1999 referendum, including one attack on a pro-independence household that resulted in the slaughter of 12 people. The incident is one of five in East Timor that are the current focus of an investigation by Indonesia's attorney general. (See "Militia Thug Eurico Guterres Leads a Charmed Life," 2000; "Militia Leader Will Be Quizzed on Dili," 2000; and "Supporters Out in Force as Guterres Appears in Court," 2001.)

[17]UNTAET was established in response to UN Security Council Resolution 1272 (October 25, 1999) with a remit to the following:

- Provide security and maintain law and order throughout the territory of East Timor
- Establish an effective administration within the province
- Assist in the development of civil and social services
- Ensure the coordination and delivery of humanitarian assistance, rehabilitation, and development aid
- Support capacity-building for the government
- Assist in the establishment of conditions for sustainable development (see McFarlane and Maley, 2001, p. 13).

[18]In July 2000, an East Timorese transitional government was established to help pave the way toward true independence. The temporary body includes former resistance leaders from the UDT and Fretilin as well as international representatives from the UN (see "Leadership Team Hailed as Vital Step," 2000).

AUSTRALIAN POLICY TO 1995

Although the violent nature of the Indonesian invasion generated widespread public animosity in Australia throughout the 1970s, 1980s and most of the 1990s, successive administrations in Canberra were prepared to support (or at least accept) Jakarta's annexation of East Timor.[19] Initially, this stance was largely influenced by a realpolitik acceptance of the incorporation of the territory as a fait accompli. However, economic prerogatives soon came to play a significant role, particularly with respect to developing and exploiting oil resources in the Timor Gap, the zone between Timor and the northwestern coast of Australia.

Canberra seemed to view that endorsing the 1975 to 1976 Indonesian occupation of East Timor would provide the Australian government with a favorable basis upon which to negotiate an extension of its continental shelf and, thereby, open up oil and gas drilling rights in that particular area.[20] Such a strategy was soon vindicated when Jakarta specifically linked the initiation of negotiations over the Timor Gap to formal recognition of its 1975 annexation. Almost immediately, therefore, a strong impetus arose in Canberra to accede to a policy of East Timorese disengagement for the sake of furthering the country's wider geostrategic imperatives (Cotton, 2000a, p. 5). As John McCredie, minister in the Australian Embassy in Jakarta, explicitly observed in a letter written to the Australian Department of Foreign Affairs in May 1974,

> Indonesian absorption of Timor makes geopolitical sense. Any other long-term solution would be potentially disruptive of both Indonesia and the region. Its [absorption] would help confirm our seabed agreement with Indonesia. It should induce a greater readiness on [Jakarta's] part to discuss Indonesia's ocean policy.[21]

In 1979, Australia granted *de jure* recognition to the Indonesian occupation of East Timor. This act of legal endorsement, the only one to be accorded by a

---

[19]In September 2000, declassified files detailing intelligence excerpts between Australia and Indonesia in 1974 to 1976 provided, for the first time, solid evidence of Canberra's complicity in Jakarta's 1975 invasion of East Timor. According to the documents, which include diplomatic cables, intelligence briefings, and ministerial advice, senior officials (including the prime minister at the time, Gough Whitlam) explicitly told Suharto that Australia viewed the incorporation of the territory as both desirable and more or less inevitable. More important, the documents also show that the Whitlam government was kept fully apprised of Indonesian plans for a forceful airborne and marine takeover and never specifically voiced its preparedness to stand in the way of such unilateral action (Monk, 2000b, and Barton, 2000; "Timor Tragedy Files Revealed Today," 2000; "Main Players Duck for Cover over Timor," 2000; "We Won't Judge Timor Action: PM," 2000; "Facing Up to a Shameful Past," 2000; "Guilty as Charged: The Timor Verdict," 2000).

[20]Between 1997 and 1998, Australia earned royalties of $1.1 million (Australian) from the recovery of oil and gas in the Timor Gap (Elang, Kakatua, and Kakatua North). (See Cotton, 1999, p. 244; "It's Time for Timor," 1999).

[21]Cited in Monk, 2000a, p. 10.

Western state, opened the way for informal talks to begin on renegotiating Australia's drilling rights off its northwestern coast. These culminated with an initial deal allowing for joint exploration of hydrocarbon deposits located in areas between the two countries' continental shelves. Upon assuming the position of foreign minister in 1988, Gareth Evans stated his determination to add further ballast to the rapidly developing Australian-Indonesian relationship; he was rewarded with the signing of the TGZCT (see Chapter Two), which was officially gazetted in February 1991 (Cotton, 2000a, pp. 7–8; Firth, 1999, pp. 195–196; McDougall, 1998, pp. 217–219).[22]

The TGZCT was important not only in terms of guaranteeing Australia a long-term share of lucrative energy supplies in the Timor Gap; it also provided a solid basis upon which to forge a meaningful and multifaceted relationship with the country's nearest and, geographically, most important regional neighbor. Such considerations took on added importance under the Labour government of Paul Keating who, as part of the general push to integrate and enmesh with Southeast Asia, placed the bilateral relationship with Indonesia above virtually all other foreign relations concerns. During his tenure as prime minister, Keating made numerous trips to the country, seeking to use the trust and confidence established by the TGZCT as a way of augmenting more complex and multifaceted links and treaty obligations in the defense and security realms.[23]

Central to Keating's Indonesian and Southeast Asia policy was a conspicuous desire to avoid confrontation over the highly sensitive East Timor issue. Indeed, even following the internationally condemned Dili Massacre, criticism was muted and within a year effectively abandoned. As McDougall notes, "Foreign Minister Garth Evans' response to this tragedy was to treat it as an aberration in Indonesian policy rather than as deriving from the nature of Indonesian rule. In this way Australia was able to treat the massacre as an 'incident' and to continue its policy towards Indonesia as before" (McDougall, 1998, p. 216; *East Timor: Report of the Senate Foreign Affairs, Defence and Trade References Committee*, 1999, p. 168).

Keating was even more explicit than Evans in his attitude toward East Timor, specifically asserting that under no circumstance was he "prepared to place

---

[22]For an overview of the main provisions of the treaty, see *East Timor: Report of the Senate Foreign Affairs, Defence and Trade References Committee*, 1999, pp. 57–59, and Bergin, 1990, pp. 383–393.

[23]See, for instance, Jones and Smith, 1999, pp. 451–452; *East Timor: Report of the Senate Foreign Affairs, Defence and Trade References Committee*, 1999, pp. 167–171; Evans and Grant, 1995, pp. 201–202. The extent of the importance with which Keating held the bilateral relationship with Jakarta was made explicit in 1992 when following meetings with President Suharto the prime minister stated that he regarded his administration as "one of the most significant and beneficial events in Australia's strategic history." He went on to affirm his commitment to "deepen the relationship and provide a greater basis of strength to it." ("PM Puts Premium on Political Stability," 1992.)

[Australia's] complex relationship with 210 million people on hold over this one issue" (Keating, 2000, p. 130; *East Timor: Report of the Senate Foreign Affairs, Defence and Trade Reference Committee*, 1999, p. 171; "The Keating Files," 2000; "Howard Faces Dilemma on E. Timor," 1999). Moreover, Keating vocally supported Suharto's argument that pushing the cause of East Timorese secessionism was liable to spark separatist sentiments elsewhere on the archipelago and could possibly lead to the wholesale balkanization of a state critical to regional stability in Southeast Asia. Keating was "rewarded" for his placatory overtones in 1995 when he and Suharto signed the AMS (Viviani, 1997, pp. 155–156; McDougall, 1998, p. 216; "How PM Has Been Working Overtime to Forge Asian Link," 1995).

AUSTRALIAN POLICY UNDER JOHN HOWARD

Within months of signing the AMS, the Labour Party lost power in national elections to a Liberal-Nationalist coalition led by John Howard. Although the new prime minister has not been as explicit in his personal overtones to Jakarta, he has remained equally as cognizant of the need to manage a stable relationship with Indonesia (see Chapter Two).[24]

Between 1996 and late 1998, this accommodationist policy—in common with Keating's policy toward Indonesia—came at the expense of adopting a more activist approach toward the East Timor issue. Such a stance held true even after the prospect of formal independence for the territory became a real possibility following Suharto's forced resignation in mid-1998. The Australian government not only repeatedly endorsed the general position that East Timor should remain an integral part of the Indonesian Republic, it also reaffirmed confidence in the unilateral ability of ABRI[25] to maintain security and order in the province. In addition, Canberra actively tried to moderate the increasingly vocal international criticism of Jakarta's centralized system of governance that was being expressed at the time (Defense officials, October 16, 2000; Dupont, 1999, p. 2).

Two main rationales were used to justify this general position of accommodating Indonesia, both of which were very much in the mold of the previous Keating legacy. First, "good" East Timor policy was equated with "good" Southeast Asian policy, namely regional engagement and enmeshment with ASEAN (which has largely dealt with the 1975 Indonesian annexation by quietly

---

[24] Howard's main criticism of Keating's policy toward Indonesia was that it was based on a personal relationship with Suharto, and not pragmatism.

[25] In 1999, ABRI changed its name to Tentara Nasional Indonesia (TNI), which some see as a symbolic gesture aimed at severing the military's past association with Suharto's New Order administration.

ignoring it and whose vigorous opposition to outside interference in the internal affairs of member states is a matter of record). Second, pressing Jakarta on the issue of self-determination was cautioned as a policy that was likely to stimulate separatism in other parts of the archipelago—namely West Kalimantan, Irian Jaya,[26] and Aceh—something that would have enormous repercussions for regional stability.[27]

By the end of 1998, however, it was apparent that a shift was beginning to occur in Australian policy and thinking. In December, Prime Minister John Howard personally wrote to Habibie urging a gradual Indonesian disengagement from East Timor, possibly along the lines of the Matigon Agreements, which had been used to resolve the situation in New Caledonia. These accords envisaged an extended period of localized self-rule (10 to 15 years) to allow for the development of viable political institutions and confidence-building so that an eventual consultation on self-determination could be held in an atmosphere of trust and honesty.[28]

Australian activism gathered apace during the first few months of 1999, particularly after Habibie's surprise announcement that he was prepared to let the East Timorese decide for themselves whether or not they wished to remain part of Indonesia. Certainly from January onward, official rhetoric in Canberra began to show an increasing preference for accelerated independence (as opposed to the earlier predilection for a prolonged period of self-rule), possibly under the initial aegis of a UN monitoring team. This more overt stance proved to be critical in helping to define negotiations between Indonesia and Portugal, which culminated with the May 1999 comprehensive agreement on East Timor and subsequent UNAMET-administered popular consultation (Cotton, 2000c; Cotton, 1999, pp. 238–239; Downer, 2000, p. 6).

It was with the civil violence that followed this ballot, however, that the true extent of the shift in Australia's Indonesia policy became most apparent. Canberra was not only one of the most vocal critics of Jakarta's inability to halt

---

[26]Irian Jaya is now known as West Papua.

[27]See, for instance, Cotton, 1999, p. 245. Like Keating, Prime Minister John Howard in the late 1990s also stressed the balkanization argument in terms of the difficulties and dangers it would raise for Australia, especially in relation to refugee flows and trade disruption.

[28]It should be noted, however, that even at this stage the Australian preference was for East Timor to remain a part of the Indonesian Republic. Nothing in Howard's letter supported the immediate assumption of independence. Rather, the idea was to give the province sweeping powers of autonomy, with full control over all areas except defense, finance, and foreign policy, and the five principles of *pancasila* that constitute Indonesia's state philosophy: a belief in one supreme god, humanism, nationalism, popular sovereignty, and social justice (Defense officials, October 16, 2000). Similar sentiments were expressed by Dr. Leonard Sebastian during interviews held at the Institute of Defense and Strategic Studies, Singapore, in October 2000. (See also Cotton, 2000b, p. 15, and *East Timor: Report of the Senate Foreign Affairs, Defence and Trade References Committee*, 1999, pp. 175–177.)

the violence in East Timor, but together with the United States it strongly pressured Jakarta to concede to the deployment of a multinational peacekeeping force to forcibly restore order in the province. ADF personnel numbering 4,500 were subsequently dispatched to East Timor as part of this effort. Until their withdrawal on February 23, 2000, they constituted the principal enforcement mechanism of UNTAET, being neither responsible to nor ultimately dependent on the wishes of the central Jakarta government (Cotton, 2000b, pp. 5–9; Huntley and Haysel, 2000, p. 5; "The East Timor Crisis," 1999, p. 1; "UN Security Council Approves East Timor Force," 1999; "As Timor Smolders, Australia Expands Its Role," 1999; "UN Plans for E. Timor Authority," 1999).

Events between late 1998 and February 2000 marked a significant departure from both John Howard's earlier and traditional Australian policy toward Indonesia and East Timor and therefore need some explanation. Several factors appeared to have played a role in encouraging the shift in Howard's thinking:

- First, assessments carried out by the Department of Foreign Affairs and Trade (DFAT) began to suggest that Indonesia could simultaneously handle its own traumatic transition toward democracy while dealing with the loss of East Timor.

- Second, a comprehensive government review, which sought the opinions of Timorese political leaders and refugees on the question of autonomy versus independence, determined that even a nominal connection to Jakarta would probably be unacceptable to the majority of the territory's population.

- Third, personal interjections by the foreign minister, Alexander Downer, fed into an increasingly active diplomatic line vis-à-vis Indonesia. Of particular importance was his insistence that, just as in Cambodia, Australia was faced with an historic opportunity to craft a resolution to a long-standing conflict, which had generated considerable political debate and interest in Australia (Cotton, 2000a, pp. 13–16).

- Finally, Habibie's totally unexpected declaration in January 1999 that a rejection of his offer of autonomy would result in separation and independence changed the entire geopolitical context of the East Timor conflict. This announcement not only provided an opening for the more activist agenda that Downer was beginning to push at the time, it also essentially presented the Australian government with a fait accompli that simply could not be ignored. In this sense, it has been suggested Canberra was simply reacting to events in Jakarta itself rather than striking out on a fundamentally different and radical East Timor policy of its own making (Australian government officials, 2000).

It was the increasingly turbulent situation that followed the August 1999 East Timor popular consultation, however, that provided the most pressing rationale for direct intervention. As one U.S. State Department official remarked, "There is a massacre quotient above which some sort of involvement inevitably has to occur" (U.S. State Department officials, 2000).

Growing revelations that much of the pro-integrationist violence was occurring with the active, or at least tacit, support of the Indonesian military merely reinforced the moral case for adopting a more active and forceful stance on the East Timor issue. Because this argument was expressed through an increasingly mobilized and media-driven public mind-set, it left Canberra with little choice but to act. In the judgment of two local experts, "No Australian government could have survived if it stood by and did nothing."

Embassy officials in Washington further believe that had there been no move to stem the violence unleashed by the pro-integrationist militias, Australia's standing as a responsible regional power would have also been severely undermined, particularly in the estimation of democratically minded nations such as the Philippines and Thailand (Foreign and political affairs officials, 2000; Huntley and Haysel, 2000, p. 5).

FALLOUT FROM AND IMPLICATIONS OF THE EAST TIMOR INTERVENTION

The most immediate impact of Australia's actions in East Timor has been felt in terms of the country's bilateral partnership with Indonesia. Relations have progressively deteriorated since the August 1999 consultation and are currently the worse they have been for three decades. Following the deployment of INTERFET, the Australian Embassy in Jakarta and Consulate General in Surabaya were targeted in mass demonstrations and calls were made by Indonesian officials to sever all diplomatic relations with Canberra (Defense officials, October 16, 2000; Indonesian foreign affairs experts, 2000; "Howard Sets Back RI-Canberra Ties," 1999; "Gun Attack on Embassy," 1999).

Although there has been no move to cut all political ties (such a move would generally be recognized as representing one of the most forceful messages of political protest one nation can send to another), the symbolically important AMS has been revoked. Several regional commentators have interpreted this act of defiance as effectively ending the peace dividend between Indonesia and Australia, placing the two countries on a functionary and possibly hostile path of escalation ("Howard Sets Back RI-Canberra Ties," 1999; "Jakarta Severs Security Ties with Canberra," 1999; "It's a Blow to Lose the Pact We Had to Have," 1999; "Pattern of Dangerous Escalation Takes Hold," 1999; "Misjudgments Will Hurt Us Too," 1999; "Democracy Marred by Mayhem,"

1999; "Partnerships the Cornerstone of Defence," 1999). As one assessment written for *The Age* newspaper in Melbourne somberly concluded:

> After investing the best part of 30 years in the diplomatic effort to cultivate a relationship of mutual respect with the power elites in Jakarta, Australians must now confront the stark unadorned truth: unless there is a systematic change governing Indonesia's political processes, there can be no genuine comity between the two countries ("A Rude Awakening: We're on Our Own," 1999).

Certainly, there is evidence to suggest that a complete lack of cordiality toward Australia now exists within Indonesia. Conspiracy theories have become increasingly rife, with both moderate and extreme politicians portraying Australia as a hegemonic middle power bent on regional aggrandizement. Canberra's 1999 intervention, especially since it was at the *head* of the INTERFET peace-keeping force, has been widely criticized as taking advantage of Jakarta's political, economic, and military weakness. Equally recent unrest in West Papua has been portrayed as a deliberately engineered Australian plan designed to further undermine stability by encouraging secession and center-region conflicts (Foreign and political affairs officials, 2000).[29]

Wider afield, Australia's ties with other Southeast Asian states have also been somewhat hurt by the East Timor episode. While these countries were not overly critical about the act of intervention itself, they did react very negatively to comments made in Australia in the immediate aftermath of the dispatch of the INTERFET forces.

Of particular note was the implied suggestion reportedly made by John Howard that Australia should not only adopt a more active role in Asian security matters, but needed to do so as a "deputy" to the United States within a wider agenda of Western-oriented interests. Although the prime minister never made any such statement himself (it was in fact a remark made by a journalist who was interviewing Howard), the fact that he took five days to distance himself from the alleged quote was widely interpreted as an implicit endorsement of its substance (Defense officials, October 16, 2000). Promptly dubbed the "Howard Doctrine," the statement was seen across the region as an indication of Canberra's preference for larger American hegemony and willingness to act as a loyal subguardian of Washington's strategic interests in the region (Sebastian, October 2000).

A barrage of criticism, especially in Malaysia, quickly followed Howard's implied suggestion of a U.S.-deputy role for Australia. Under Prime Minister

---

[29]Similar sentiments were expressed to me during interviews conducted with Australian defense officials and experts in Jakarta and Canberra in October and December 2000 (see also "Howard Sets Back RI-Canberra Ties," 1999).

Mahathir Mohamad, Malaysia has become progressively more suspicious and hostile to Canberra's liberal democratic identity,[30] and repeated accusations were made in Malaysia that Australia was pursuing an aggressive and possibly hidden agenda in East Timor. Even erstwhile allies such as Thailand dismissed Howard's alleged statement as "inappropriate" and at odds with the normative realities of a region in which both memories of European colonialism and preferences for consensual and nonintrusive modes of interstate diplomacy remained particularly strong (Milner, 2000, p. 179; "Howard Still Under Fire in Asia over Regional Policy," 1999; "Australia Must Know Its Place," 2000; "East Timor Crisis Heralds Change in ASEAN and Regional Power Struggles," 1999; "Anger in Asia as Australia Searches for New Regional Role," 1999; "Asian Media Criticizes Australia's Role in East Timor," 1999).

Although Howard repeatedly asserted that he never personally made the "deputy" remark, his implied endorsement of its content left an indelible impression. This was perhaps best reflected by the huge diplomatic effort, involving all of Australia's Southeast Asian embassies, that had to be organized to assure governments of the region that the East Timor intervention represented a wholly unique circumstance, and was not a defining template for future strategic doctrine ("Howardism," 1999).

Apart from these regional diplomatic considerations, the East Timor intervention has also had significant implications for Australian defense policy, not the least by graphically demonstrating the limitations of Canberra's offshore force projection capacities. Although INTERFET did not require the deployment of all of the ADF's assets, those that were marshaled were stretched to the limit. Indeed, it is generally recognized that had the operation necessitated another three to four months' commitment, the military would have faced enormous, and possibly insurmountable, problems in sustaining peacekeeping efforts and enforcing activities on the ground, particularly had they been contested by the

---

[30]Several factors have played into the increasingly turbulent Malaysian-Australian relationship over the past ten years:

- The institutionalization of Islam in the Malaysian polity, which has caused the country to be especially sensitive to Australian liberal attitudes and values.

- The screening in 1990 of an Australian television series titled *The Embassy*, which was perceived in Kuala Lumpur as presenting a disparaging view of Malaysia.

- Keating's reference to Mahathir's "recalcitrant" attitude in 1993 after the Malaysian leader failed to attend a meeting of APEC leaders in Seattle.

- Howard's strong endorsement of the Australian-U.S. relationship since 1996, which has reinforced the Malaysian attitude that Canberra neither wishes to be nor should be recognized as integral to the Southeast Asian (or, indeed, wider Asia-Pacific) regional community.

- Howard's failure to distance his government from Pauline Hanson's One Nation Party after it gained representation in the Australian Parliament in 1996 on a largely anti-Asian, quasi-racist agenda.

TNI (Dupont, 2000c).[31] Defense officials freely admit this, conceding that perhaps one of the most important lessons to come out of East Timor is the ADF's current inability to mount long-term low-end operations with appropriate sealift/airlift and logistical support (Foreign and political affairs officials, 2000).[32]

Whereas part of this situation is seen to be a factor of insufficient government spending, it is now also increasingly regarded as an inevitable product of defense priorities that have had little relevance for the type of contingencies the ADF is most likely to face. The combined emphasis on the RMA and "conventional war" assets, to both protect the so-called air-sea gap to Australia's north and facilitate interoperability with United States forces for alliance commitments in distant Northeast Asian theaters, is deemed to have been particularly important in this regard (Bergin, 2000; Woodman, 2000).[33]

Therefore, in looking to the future, three principal issues would appear to be evident for the Australian policymaking community:

- First, the foreign policy challenge of how to rebuild the badly damaged bilateral relationship with Indonesia, which remains the natural bridge to wider Southeast Asian engagement

- Second, how to reconfigure the ADF in such a manner that its resources are best matched to deal with the type of contingencies the country is most likely to face without thereby raising the concerns of regional nations

- Third, the question of how to ensure the continued viability of the Australian-U.S. defense partnership, particularly in light of the current Bush administration, which explicitly emphasizes the notion of coalition warfare and alliance commitments.

I address these interrelated themes in Chapters Four and Five.

---

[31]Similar sentiments were expressed by Dr. Anthony Bergin during interviews held at the Australian Defence Studies Centre (ADSC), Australian Defence Force Academy (ADFA), in December 2000.

[32]Similar points were emphasized by defense experts during discussions at the Australian Embassy in Jakarta on October 16, 2000.

[33]Similar sentiments were expressed by Alan Dupont during interviews at the Strategic and Defence Studies Centre (SDSC), Australian National University (ANU), on September 12, 2000.

Chapter Four

AUSTRALIAN-INDONESIAN RELATIONS: MENDING THE RIFT AND STRENGTHENING TIES

Australia's leading role in the September 1999 INTERFET intervention has undoubtedly had a major deleterious effect on the Jakarta-Canberra relationship, which is currently the worst that it has been since the period of *konfrontasi* in the 1960s. This chapter explores the current nature of the impasse and discusses means to rebuild and stabilize relations, including the two nations' defense ties.

THE AUSTRALIAN-INDONESIAN IMPASSE

Symbolically, the deteriorated relationship between Canberra and Jakarta was most visibly expressed by the abrogation of the AMS in September 1999, with Feisal Tandjung, Indonesia's Coordinating Minister for Political and Security Affairs, specifically asserting that Australia's actions in East Timor were inconsistent with both the letter and spirit of the treaty agreement ("Indonesia Scraps Security Treaty over East Timor," 1999; "Jakarta Severs Security Ties with Canberra," 1999; "It's a Blow to Lose the Pact We Had to Have," 1999; "Pattern of Dangerous Escalation Takes Hold," 1999). Since then, relations have continued to deteriorate amid a surge of national sentiment, which has targeted Australian expatriates in Java and outlying provinces as well as diplomatic missions in Jakarta and Surabaya ("History Binds Indonesia and Australia," 1999; "Howard Sets Back RI-Canberra Ties," 1999).

One particularly serious incident occurred in November 2000 when the Australian ambassador to Indonesia, John McCarthy, was attacked and placed in personal danger by a rioting crowd of several dozen pro-Jakarta protesters. According to diplomatic sources, the Indonesian police deliberately failed to contain the incident, which occurred during the opening of an Australian insurance office in Mahassa, southern Sulawesi ("Indonesian Protesters Attack Australian Ambassador," 2000).

Very much indicative of the poor state of relations between the two countries has been the severance of virtually all high-level governmental and official contacts. Military-military (mil-mil) links—including joint training and exercises, both of which were extremely strong prior to the East Timor crisis—have been curtailed and show no sign of being resumed in the near future. Ministerial relations have also been reduced to the most basic level of common interest and certainly do not embrace anywhere near the range of issues that were commonplace during the 1990s (Cotton, 2000c).

For many Indonesians, Australia's actions in East Timor were tantamount to a betrayal of trust from what had hitherto been a very close and supportive friend. Having been one of the few countries to have explicitly recognized Indonesian sovereignty over East Timor and having consistently backed Jakarta's position in the province since 1976, it was regarded as particularly irksome that Canberra should have been at the forefront of moves that eventually led to East Timor's independence (*East Timor: Report of the Senate Foreign Affairs, Defence and Trade References Committee*, 1999, pp. 195–196; "Jakarta's Simmering Anger over Timor," 2000; "Howard Sets Back RI-Canberra Ties," 1999; "Indonesia-Australia Ties: What Went Wrong?" 1999). The fact that these moves occurred when Indonesia was already experiencing considerable internal social, political, and economic[1] difficulties only served to fuel national misgivings. In the words of one analyst, "Australia became a very bad friend at a very bad time."[2]

Further exacerbating local discontent in Indonesia are entrenched suspicions that Australia deliberately orchestrated the popular consultation in East Timor and is now seeking to encourage secessionism in other parts of Indonesia. On the one hand, there has been a tendency (albeit an incorrect one) to equate the policies of the central Australian government with the actions of independent human rights activists and lobbyists who have called for greater international mediation in areas such as Aceh and Irian Jaya. Just as significantly, there has been an assumption that Australia (and the international community in general) will *inevitably* come to support independence in Irian Jaya simply because it is Christian, which is itself a misapplied lesson from the East Timor experience. Significantly, these views have been embraced and aired not only by hard-liners in the TNI but also by senior politicians in Jakarta, including two

---

[1] It should be noted that Jim Wolfensohn, president of the World Bank and also representative to Indonesia and an Australian, was very much seen in Jakarta as having "ganged up" with others in regard to East Timor during the August–September 1999 crisis.

[2] The analyst made the comment during the Indonesia-Australia Forum (IASFOR) meeting in Canberra on November 22, 2000.

successive ministers of defense, Juwono Sudarsono and Mohamad Mahfud (Defense officials, October 16, 2000; Foreign and political affairs officials, 2000).[3]

The practical effect of these perceptions has been to underscore Australia as, at best, a peripheral and, at worst, an actively hostile state that is seeking to undermine Indonesia's stability and position in Southeast Asia. Indeed, the idea that Canberra constitutes merely a "regional appendix," which should be neither recognized nor embraced as part of the wider Southeast Asian family, has begun to take on added currency in Indonesia to the extent that it now forms official *dictat* among certain government officials and ministries.

One of the key challenges that has emerged for Australia, therefore, is how to rebuild a positive partnership with Indonesia, which avoids possible pitfalls that could further strain bilateral relations. Such an undertaking is important for at least three reasons:

- First, Indonesia constitutes Australia's largest and most immediate regional neighbor. As such, it necessarily occupies a crucial place in foreign policy and defense calculations. The existence of an openly antagonistic nation so close to Australia's shores is something that no government would seek to court, let alone countenance, through active indifference.

- Second, a stable relationship will allow Canberra to play a constructive role in Indonesia's future development, which will in itself contribute to peace and stability in the so-called Inner Arc surrounding Australia's northern approaches.

- Third, Indonesia remains an important conduit to Southeast Asia. Although it is true that the country's regional standing has suffered over the past few years as a result of pressing internal problems, Jakarta continues to form the linchpin of ASEAN and its associated forums. This abiding influence is something that can be used forcefully either in support of or against Canberra's wider engagement efforts, particularly given lingering concerns in several Southeast Asian capitals over the way in which Australia was perceived to have presented its intervention in East Timor—that is, as a "deputy" of the United States.

---

[3]Similar views were expressed by Dr. Suzaine Kadir during interviews conducted at the National University of Singapore (NUS) on October 19, 2000.

REBUILDING INDONESIAN-AUSTRALIAN RELATIONS: WHAT TYPE OF PARTNERSHIP?

It is extremely unlikely that Australian-Indonesian relations will return to the heady days of the Keating era, at least in the short or medium term.[4] Not only were the very close contacts that existed at that time largely a product of the personal affinity between the Australian premier and President Suharto, the fallout from the East Timor intervention has also fundamentally transformed the way in which both states view one another. In particular, it has destroyed the notion that Jakarta and Canberra necessarily need to engage on the basis of a uniquely "special" partnership. The future Australian-Indonesian relationship will almost certainly be founded on practicalities rather than sentiment, where working together is seen as a matter of necessity and propinquity, and not necessarily coming from the heart (Defense officials, October 16, 2000).

This current state of affairs obviously will not lend itself to the type of unprecedented cordiality that characterized the Australian-Indonesian partnership during much of the 1990s, and particularly between 1990 and 1995. One of the remarkable features of that period was the inability of what would have been major diplomatic land mines, under normal circumstances, to upset the course of wider bilateral relations (Evans and Grant, 1995, p. 204). This was, perhaps, best reflected by the marginal damage wrought by the 1991 Dili Massacre (see Chapter Three), although the limited fallout following Prime Minister John Howard's failure to quickly denounce the anti-Asian agenda of Pauline Hanson after her One Nation Party rose to prominence in 1996 provides another good example ("Ambivalence Serves Only to Marginalise Us," 1996; "When Change Calls for Consistency," *1996*; "A Case of Regional Identity," 1996).

In the absence of "sentimental ballast" such as that just described, it will be far easier for disputes and controversies—both major and minor—to have a prominent and direct impact on bilateral relations. The key for Canberra over the next few years will be to shape policies that constructively build on those diplomatic openings that do exist, while moving to ensure that potential pitfalls, of which there are many, do not escalate to assume unwarranted significance and importance on the bilateral agenda.

---

[4]It is conceivable that through sustained diplomacy, and with improved economic prospects and a new generation of political leaders, a renewed relationship will emerge akin to that of the Keating-Suharto era. At the time of writing, however, there was little, if any, sign of such developments taking place.

STABILIZING AUSTRALIAN-INDONESIAN RELATIONS: BASIC BUILDING BLOCKS

Restoring some semblance of stability to the Australian-Indonesian relationship will take time. Indeed, some commentators have suggested that it may take as long as 10 years before a fully constructive partnership re-emerges. While this may be somewhat of an overstatement, the chaotic economic and political situation that currently besets Indonesia undoubtedly works against a rapid resumption of ties. The most significant problem in this regard is the lack of strong centralized leadership in Jakarta.

During his tenure as Indonesian president (1999–2001), Abdurrahman Wahid successfully managed to undermine much of his political capital through an erratic style of governance characterized by off-the-cuff comments, abrupt changes in policy direction, and impulsive and largely unnecessary cabinet reshuffling (Barton, 2000; Emerson, 2000, pp. 103–104; "Talking About a Devolution," 2001). Alluding to these unpredictable leadership tendencies and character traits, Amien Rais, the chair of the People's Consultative Assembly (MPR) in Jakarta, somewhat cynically remarked, "[For Indonesians] there are three mysteries in life: when they are going to die, the weather, and what their president is going to say or do next."[5]

In July 2001, the Indonesian National Assembly overwhelmingly voted to remove Wahid for his poor performance, attitude, and policies, replacing him with Vice President Megawati Sukarnoputri ("Megawati Makes Her Move," 2001; "Indonesian President Voted Out," 2001). It is unclear, however, whether the change of leaderhip will do anything to stabilize the political situation in Jakarta. Indeed, analysts, politicians, and regional comentators have already expressed serious reservations over Megawati, questioning her skill, intellect, instincts, and even her inclination to lead the country. In particular, they appear to doubt her ability to manage the myriad problems Indonesia currently faces, which range from a corrupt and dysfunctional civil service to a badly faltering economy, ongoing separatist tensions, and a demoralized (but still highly dangerous) security apparatus (Indonesian foreign affairs experts, 2000; "Megawati Makes her Move," 2001; "Indonesian President Voted Out," 2001).[6]

The situation just described has served to obfuscate the clarity of Canberra's future strategy in Indonesia, not least because it has made it difficult to know what sort of relationships to establish and with whom to build them. As Professor James Cotton of the ADFA observes, Australia will almost certainly

---

[5] Cited in Emerson, 2000, p. 103.

[6] For a good overview of many of these problems see Emerson, 2000; Sulong, 2000; Collison, 2000; and "Indonesia Is in Danger of Coming Apart," 2000.

have to wait for things to settle down in Indonesia and for the country to sort itself out before any substantive progress on rebuilding ties can begin (Cotton, 2000c).

This being said, there are certain things that can be done to help promote a stable future working relationship. Most important, Australia can seek to engage Indonesia in areas of common interest. Several commentators have highlighted East Timor as representing one issue on which to concentrate in this regard. It has been suggested, for instance, that a "triangular" partnership be established to deal with such things as seabed resource allocations, refugee resettlement, investigations of human rights violations and atrocities, and the control of militias that continue to operate from West Timor (Sebastian, 2000; Downer, 2000, pp. 9–10; Klitgaard, 2001). Certainly these areas are important. However, it is probably too soon for Australia and Indonesia to attempt to work together on such substantive matters, largely because Canberra's role in the INTERFET intervention remains an extremely raw issue in Jakarta, which has left little room for meaningful diplomatic bargaining and negotiation to take place on sensitive issues related to East Timor and its recent past. This was specifically recognized by both Indonesian and Australian analysts attending a two-day forum on bilateral confidence-building measures (CBMs) held in Canberra in November 2000 (Cotton, 2000c).

A more realistic approach would be for Australia to undertake initiatives designed to bolster East Timorese self-sufficiency and ensure the territory's long-term viability. This would be very much to the advantage of Indonesia and, hopefully, appreciated as such. As Alan Dupont observes:

> A weak and chronically unstable East Timor could present opportunities for unwelcome external power involvement by states with radical ideologies or anti-Western leanings—precisely the outcome that [Jakarta] has always feared. . . . [Equally] there is a . . . risk that poverty, intercommunal tensions and entrenched political violence could lead to social unrest, which would inevitably spill over East Timor's borders, creating friction with Indonesia and other states (Dupont, 2000b).

Many political observers remain skeptical of Dili's long-term socioeconomic viability and doubt Australia's capacity to foster a polity that will not become another Melanesian dependent. Several factors are commonly noted in this regard. On assuming full independence, East Timor will become one of the poorest countries in the world; more than 40 percent of the population currently live on less than $1 (U.S.) a day, and overall per-capita income is estimated at only $400 (U.S.) a year. Most of the indigenous infrastructure was completely destroyed by pro-integrationist militias in the aftermath of the August 1999 popular consultation and will have to be rebuilt. The economy is based on a very narrow resource base—primarily Arabica coffee beans, sandalwood, and fish—and is essentially being sustained on "artificial" influxes of money generated by the large numbers of UN personnel currently stationed in the territory (Defense officials, December 15, 2000; Dupont, 2000a, p. 169; Klitgaard, 2001, p. 5; "Square One," 2000; "Australia's Acid Test at the Bottom of the Timor Sea," 2000; "Timor's Troubled Waters," 2000).

In many ways, however, the prospects for East Timor are not as grim as the preceding prognosis suggests. There remains in place a fairly strong civil society, far more so than that of Cambodia following the end of the Third Indochina War. One indicator of this is the relative lack of prostitution, despite the existence of a (UN) cash economy and the presence of peacekeeping troops prone to periods of inactivity and boredom.[7]

In addition, both the World Bank and Asian Development Bank have indicated that generous development aid will be forthcoming. Based on grants provided by international aid agencies to Mozambique and Eritrea, assistance levels could run to as much as $100 million (U.S.) per year after the emergency phase is over (Klitgaard, 2001). This will provide much needed financial breathing space for the new government to begin rebuilding infrastructure and diversifying into other areas of potential economic activity such as tourism, agribusiness, and oil and gas exploration in the Timor Gap ("Perky Future," 1999; "Economy of Scale," 1999).[8]

Reflecting on these positive facets, Australia has declared that it is fully ready to support East Timor's transition to independence, pledging, along with Japan and Portugal, to underwrite the territory's short-term financial future (Dupont, 2000b). The Howard government has also committed $28 million (Australian) over the next five years in defense assistance, most of which will be used to help raise an independent East Timorese army ("$26m Fund for Timor Rebel Force," 2000; "East Timor to Raise Army," 2000; "Timor's Troubled Waters," 2000).

There are many other areas in which Canberra can and ought to play a useful and constructive role, not the least in terms of helping to provide resolute and efficient systems for law and order, criminal justice, education, training, and general civil administration—all vital components of any functioning sovereign

---

[7]This point was specifically emphasized by James Cotton during interviews at the ADFA in December 2000.

[8]Estimates of the value of oil below the Timor Gap vary. However, the three main reserves at Sunrise-Troubadour, Bayu-Undan and Elang-Kakatua, are projected to contain a total of 500 million barrels, which is worth roughly $17 billion (U.S.) at today's prices. Under the original provisions of the Timor Gap Treaty, 50 percent of this income would have gone to East Timor (with the remaining half going to Australia). On July 3, 2001, however, Canberra agreed to a revised formula providing for a 90–10 revenue split in favor of Dili (see "Australia's Acid Test at the Bottom of the Timor Sea," 2000; "Timor's Troubled Waters," 2000, and "Australia Sees Reason," 2001).

entity.[9] By fostering development in these key sectors, Australia will be laying important groundwork for Dili's future integration and security within ASEAN. This will both contribute to peace and stability along Indonesia's southern rim and help to ensure that East Timor acts as a bridge (rather than an obstacle) to relations between Canberra and Jakarta within the wider Southeast Asian community (Dupont, 2000c).

The key challenge for Canberra will be to clearly articulate, both in actions and words, its intentions in East Timor. Above all, the government must convey the message that ties to Jakarta come first and that the purpose of facilitating Dili's long-term rehabilitation is to foster peace and stability for the good of Australia, Indonesia, and the region. This will require an incremental policy approach that necessarily involves trade-offs between the strident pursuit of politically sensitive goals (such as human rights investigations) and the advancement of more neutral socioeconomic and institutional objectives.

Aside from East Timor, Australia must also actively look for opportunities where it can further its involvement in and with Indonesia itself. Clearly Canberra will have to tread lightly here and avoid overtures that are likely to be perceived as overly meddlesome or imperialistic. Obviously, initiatives that seek to address sensitive internal issues such as human rights and corruption will have to wait until a more consistent and solid basis has been established for bilateral contacts. However, there are several CBMs that could be instituted, which would help to not only break the diplomatic ice presently existing between Jakarta and Canberra but, more importantly, lock into place norms and procedures for future engagement and deliberations.

At the most basic level, Australia could help to promote more intensive (and constructive) person-to-person links through tourism and educational exchanges and by fostering an active program of track-two diplomacy. These contacts proved to be an important element of the stable Australian-Indonesian partnership during the 1990s and could be effectively used to mitigate some of the "conspiranoia" that is currently besetting bilateral relations (especially at the academic and journalist level).[10] In addition, Canberra could usefully contribute to Indonesia's economic development and restructuring both directly by providing aid and assistance and indirectly by acting as an intermedi-

---

[9]McFarlane and Maley argue that the reconstitution of law and order and the criminal justice sector is especially important in the early stages of stabilizing a fragmented state, particularly in terms of moving the polity away from a military toward a civilian political system (see McFarlane and Maley, 2001).

[10]Comments to this effect were made by Indonesian delegates attending the IASFOR meeting in Canberra in November 2000.

ary between Jakarta and international financial institutions such as the World Bank and the IMF.

On a diplomatic front, Australia should be more systematic about reaching out to the various moderate factions that continue to hold sway in Indonesia, especially in terms of emphasizing the many mutual benefits that can result from increased bilateral functional contacts and cooperation. Canberra could also think seriously about issuing a joint statement with Jakarta affirming Indonesian sovereignty over the Natuna Islands in the South China Sea. As Professor William Tow of the University of Queensland observes, this would be a good public relations move in the sense that it would be sure to generate a favorable response in Jakarta (Tow, 2001). Moreover, it is an action that is unlikely to have a negative impact on Australia's other relations in Southeast Asia (with the possible exception of Vietnam, which might view this as a threat to its demarcation line on the continental shelf in the South China Sea) (Manning, 1996, p. 25; Ball, 1993/1994, pp. 88–89).

Perhaps the most important thing that the Howard government could do, however, is to help develop CBMs for Irian Jaya and Aceh, the two most restive provinces in Indonesia today. Canberra has already gone to extraordinary lengths to affirm its unambiguous support for Jakarta's territorial integrity and to make it clear that the government supports the independence aspirations of neither Gerakan Aceh Merdeka (GAM) or the Free Papua Movement (OPM) (Department of Defence, December 2000; "Rebel Says Australian Stance a Terrible Mistake," 2000). It is essential, however, that Australia demonstrates a practical commitment to this rhetoric by working to develop concrete measures specifically designed to dampen centrifugal tendencies and pressures. These should be finessed in conjunction with Indonesia, possibly via the track-two diplomatic process noted earlier in this section, and could include such areas as devolution, resource sharing/allocation, and law and order (particularly with regard to TNI deployments).

The importance of developing viable CBMs on Aceh and particularly Irian Jaya should not be underestimated. A major outbreak of mass violence in either province would undoubtedly generate significant public pressure in Australia for some sort of stabilizing intervention, which Canberra would be extremely hard-pressed to ignore (Cotton, 2000c). If unrest broke out in Irian Jaya, there would be the added complication of Papua New Guinea (PNG), a nation that Australia is treaty-bound to defend. Such an obligation could present numerous difficulties, particularly if the fighting escalated and spilled over into PNG territory (Defense officials, December 15, 2000).

Any actual dispatch of ADF assets as a result of these types of considerations would be catastrophic in terms of Canberra's relationship with Indonesia. Not only would Jakarta be sure to interpret such a deployment as evidence of wider Australian territorial designs, but unlike with East Timor, there would also be a strong likelihood of the operation being contested by the TNI and, thereby, coming to involve a substantial number of military casualties and deaths. The prospects for a renewal of ties under such circumstances would be negligible, quite possibly destroying *any* chance for an Indonesian-Australian rapprochement (Monk, 2000b).[11]

The physical institution of these building blocks will obviously require Indonesia to meet Australia halfway. Above all, officials in Jakarta will have to accept at face value that Canberra has no wish or desire to destroy the Indonesian Republic's territorial integrity and to refrain from grounding policies and assessments on unfounded and speculative forecasts. Indeed, until this occurs, everything that Australia does to improve bilateral relations will be held captive to Indonesian suspicions of the country's "true" intentions, formed not on the basis of what has or is happening but around predictions over what will *apparently* happen.

Just as important, there needs to be a more honest assessment and frank appreciation of the events surrounding the East Timor intervention itself. Jakarta has to accept the failure of its past policies in the province and recognize that the majority of East Timor's inhabitants neither saw themselves, nor wished to be considered as, part of Indonesia. It was this unwillingness to integrate that ultimately led to the vote against autonomy (which, itself, was a product of a decision made in Jakarta) and not some grand geostrategic scheme cooked up in the defense halls of Canberra. Moreover, there has to be an appreciation of the liberal democratic character that underscores Australian political society and the fact that this ethos simply would not have tolerated inaction in response to the civil violence that was unleashed following the 1999 consultation.

AUSTRALIAN-INDONESIAN DEFENSE TIES

As noted earlier in this chapter, Australian-Indonesian defense relations have been undermined as a result of the INTERFET intervention. This is true both in terms of policy—as reflected by the termination of the AMS—and working partnerships. Indeed, other than occasional low-level military educational and staff college exchanges, no physical military-military links currently exist between the two countries, including security components that were common

---

[11]Similar points were raised by Alan Dupont during interviews at the SDSC, ANU in Canberra on September, 12, 2000.

during the 1990s such as land-force exercises and Special Forces (SF) training (Scrafton, 1999, p. 854; White, 2000, p. 88).

For Jakarta, the cessation of these contacts has largely been a product of the ill will generated by the fallout from the East Timor crisis. For Canberra, however, the reduced emphasis on maintaining concerted mil-mil links has had more to do with ongoing concerns about professionalism within the TNI, particularly in terms of respect for human rights and related internal security duties.

Australian apprehensions pertaining to the Indonesian military were initially aroused following widespread allegations of direct army involvement in the wave of pro-integrationist violence that accompanied East Timor's independence transition, both before and after the August 1999 consultation (see Chapter Three). Concerns over the TNI have since been entrenched by confirmation of this complicity (at least with respect to certain army units), along with evidence that SF elements continue to assist militia attacks on refugee camps in West Timor and remain predisposed to the use of heavy-handed tactics against groups such as GAM and OPM (*East Timor: Report of the Senate Foreign Affairs Defence and Trade References Committee*, 1999, pp. 201–207; "New Military Ties with Indonesia in Sight," 2000; "Aust. Cancels Military Training with Indonesia," 1999).

It has been suggested that Australia should seek to re-engage Indonesia in the defense realm, both as a useful CBM that would have beneficial political spin-offs and as a way of helping Jakarta create a viable and effective military structure. Moreover, ADF planners argue that because any attack on the Australian mainland would have to be staged through the Indonesian archipelago, the restoration of military ties is a matter of practical urgency as it would help to create a positive strategic shield to the north (Dupont, 2000c).

A resumption of military ties has also been defended on the grounds that the close cooperation and baseline relationship established between the ADF and Indonesian army units during the 1990s had major benefits during the East Timor crisis and were among the main factors accounting for the uncontested nature of the INTERFET deployment (Defense officials, October 16, 2000).[12] According to Major General Peter Cosgrove who led the intervention force,

> I believe there was a pay-off there through an understanding, hopefully some level of respect, which defused [the] situation that could have been much more critical. They predisposed protagonists from my level down to talk through issues rather than to shoot through them. Maybe our astonishingly low casualty

---

[12]Australian officials have also stressed that the TNI and especially the Indonesian Police Mobile Brigades (BRIMOB) played a valuable role protecting and assisting UNAMET personnel in the period leading up to the August 1999 popular consultation (McFarlane, 2001).

count . . . is to some degree testimony to that factor. [Specifically, two benefits derived from the military relationship.] First, TNI had a clear view of our competence and determination and, secondly, I'm convinced that from time to time personal relationships and mutual respect had pay-offs in minimising and resolving misunderstandings at the level of our troops' interaction.[13]

Notwithstanding the various considerations noted here, it is unlikely that a full resumption of military ties will occur in the near future (assuming that Jakarta would even agree to this in the first place). The involvement of SF units and certain elements of the TNI in the humanitarian crisis that broke out in East Timor is now a matter of record, even if it did not involve the full Indonesian military apparatus. This, together with ongoing concerns over army-militia links in West Timor and internal security operations in Aceh and Irian Jaya,[14] has prevented any broad political consensus from emerging in Canberra that countenances a rapid restoration of the defense program.[15]

Wariness of re-establishing concerted mil-mil links is particularly true of SF contacts, largely because specialist units trained by the Australian Special Air Service (SAS), such as Kopassus, Detachment-81 (the army's main antiterrorist squad) and KOSTRAD, have been the ones most closely identified with human rights abuses in East Timor and elsewhere. Currently, very little support exists for re-instituting links with these organizations and the general consensus in Australia is that should training exchanges eventually be resuscitated the focus must be on defense (rather than internal security)[16] and only provided after a process of careful vetting.[17]

---

[13]Cosgrove, cited in "Indonesian Defence Ties Helped in Timor Crisis," 2000, and "Ties with Indonesian Military Prevented Bloodshed: Cosgrove," 2000.

[14]Indonesian officials concede that internal security operations in Aceh and Irian Jaya, and other outlying regions such as Kalimantan and the Moluccas, remain issues of concern, particularly in terms of arbitrary detentions, torture, and the use of live ammunition to disperse protest crowds (Security and foreign affairs analysts, Center for Political and Area Studies, October 16, 2000; see also "Human Rights and Pro-Independence Actions in Papua, 1999-2000," 2000; Ravich, 2000, pp. 13–15; Chalk, 2000b, pp. 1–2; Aspinall, 2000, pp. 6–7; Tiwon, 2000; Dolven, 2000; Murphy, 2000; Djalal, 2000).

[15]Comments to this effect were made by delegates attending the Indonesia-Australia Track Two Forum (IASFOR) meeting in Canberra on November 22, 2000.

[16]It should be noted that several defense officials reject the argument that the SAS was involved in internal security training for Indonesian SFs. For instance, in testifying before the Senate Foreign Affairs, Defence and Trade References Committee in November 1999, Michael Scrafton, head of the Department of Defence's East Timor Policy Unit, stated, "In terms of the Indonesian army and specifically the most contentious element, Kopassus, the training has been very specific. The intention of the training with Kopassus and the Indonesian army has been in two major areas—primarily about basic military skills training. It is nothing to do with insurgency training or managing internal security issues, but primarily in the areas of basic training and infantry skills" (*East Timor: Report of the Senate Foreign Affairs, Defence and Trade References Committee*, 1999, p. 203).

[17]See, for instance, "East Timor Hearings," September 20, 1999, p. 583.

Very much indicative of the present (political) aversion in Canberra to rapidly reinstituting a comprehensive program of defense cooperation with Indonesia is the *Senate Foreign Affairs, Defence and Trade References Committee's 2000 Report on East Timor*. Published just before Christmas 2000, the report specifically argued against a prompt renewal of substantive military contacts, stressing that no moves should be made in that direction until two broad criteria had been met. These qualifying conditions—and their rationalization—are important and worth quoting in full:

> The first criterion is a resolution of the refugee problem in West Timor and the neutralisation of the East Timorese militias, including preventions of their incursions into East Timor. While the TNI abrogates its responsibilities in West Timor and fails to comply fully with [the] Indonesian Government relating to refugees and militias, it is not in the interests of Australia, East Timor or other countries involved in the rebuilding of East Timor after the ravages of the militias and TNI in September 1999 for Australia to provide defence cooperation with Indonesia. It would almost be tantamount to condoning TNI actions during and after the destruction.

> The second criterion is clear evidence that the TNI is dismantling the territorial command structure throughout Indonesia and that it is becoming a professional defence force rather than mainly an internal security force. It has been the territorial command structure that has given the TNI the power to meddle in domestic matters both nationally and right down to village levels, and given rise to gross human rights abuses perpetrated in East Timor and elsewhere in Indonesia (*East Timor: Report of the Senate Foreign Affairs, Defence and Trade References Committee*, 1999, p. 207).[18]

Whereas a full resumption of the Australian-Indonesian defense program remains unrealistic at this stage (neither of the conditions just listed is likely to be met quickly), there is scope for more limited cooperation. As previously noted, periodic educational activities and staff college level exchanges continue to take place, which could be expanded and further consolidated, both in their own right and as part of the broader person-to-person effort outlined earlier. Such

---

[18]Some changes are beginning to occur within Indonesia with respect to civil-military relations, including the following:

- The full separation of the police from the armed forces

- The establishment of an independent structure and legal framework for the police, which will now act as a fully civilian (rather than paramilitary) force with sole responsibility for internal security (formerly the preserve of the military)

- Reduced military representation in Parliament (which, theoretically, is to be phased out altogether by 2009)

- Increased civilian control over the military, through the appointment of two non-TNI defense ministers, Juwono Sudarsono and Mohamad Mahfud (Mandane, 2001).

At the time of this writing, however, the TNI territorial structure remained very much in place, with 17 regional commands, down to the village level, in existence.

contacts will be helpful not only in terms of facilitating mutual trust and understanding between Australian and Indonesian officers, they will also provide a useful mechanism for furthering greater human development, and thereby professionalism, within the TNI.

Canberra and Jakarta could also usefully collaborate in addressing proximate "soft" nontraditional military threats such as piracy and unregulated population movements. The magnitude of these problems has greatly increased in recent years, their scope and incidence driven by the general climate of social instability in Indonesia that has encouraged unsolicited migration, exacerbated official corruption, and fed a proliferating parallel economy powered by both land-based and sea-based illicit activities. Further complicating the situation has been the difficulty of effectively securing the expansive Indonesian coastline, something that has been made no less difficult by the lack of resources Jakarta has been able to devote to the maritime realm since 1997—the year when the country's financial crisis first started to take hold (Chalk, 2000a, pp. 70–71; Dupont, 1997; "Australia Targets the Boat People," 2000).

Considerable scope exists for practical Australian assistance in helping to regulate these "gray area" phenomena, particularly with regard to proactive intelligence exchanges, the provision of coastal surveillance technologies, and the institution of joint patrols to secure strategic sea-lanes of communication (SLOCs) (Tow, 2001). Collaboration of this sort would benefit both countries, given that human smuggling and piracy in contiguous regions such as the Torres Strait and Arafura Sea have as many implications for Canberra as they do for Jakarta. Moreover, cooperation in "soft security" matters would also act as a useful "first base" from which to re-institutionalize more traditional defense links and ties when, and if, such moves become politically acceptable.[19]

Little question exists that significant challenges lie ahead in terms of repairing the Australian-Indonesian relationship, particularly given the suspicion and instability that continues to underscore the political climate in Jakarta. However, with careful and deft management, there is no reason why a renewed partnership built on transparency, reliability, and consistency should not eventually develop. While this partnership will almost certainly lack the mutual empathy of the Keating era (at least in the near to medium term), it will provide the basis for a more businesslike and frank style of political engagement. Not only will this type of partnership give a somewhat more honest character to the bilateral Australian-Indonesian links, it should also help to prevent latent sources of tension from festering into long-term and possibly intractable problems.

---

[19]Observations to this effect were made by delegates attending the IASFOR meeting in Canberra on November 22, 2000.

Chapter Five

EXAMINING AUSTRALIA'S DEFENSE CAPABILITIES
IN LIGHT OF EAST TIMOR

As I concluded in Chapter Three, the implications of the East Timor crisis went well beyond Canberra's relationship with Indonesia. Just as important were the lessons that it highlighted in terms of Australian defense assets and priorities.

The deployment of the INTERFET force was the largest and most demanding mission undertaken by the Australian military since the Vietnam War. Whereas the ADF received a good deal of credit for the way the peacekeeping intervention was subsequently carried out, significant questions were also raised concerning the ability of the defense forces to sustain the full range of their capabilities at appropriate levels of sophistication and readiness given the present resources. In particular, the East Timor deployment generated concerns that a mismatch had developed between Australia's strategic objectives, its defense assets, and its levels of defense spending.

During the 1990s, the relatively benign post–Cold War Southeast Asian environment led to a neglect of the ADF, both in terms of financial expenditures and human resources. By the time of the INTERFET intervention, for instance, the overall size of the ADF had declined by nearly 30 percent from 1990 figures, which was largely a product of the $100 billion (U.S.) shortfall that had accrued in defense funding since 1987.[1] Defense investments, to the extent that they were made, were largely aimed at maintaining a small and streamlined conventional fighting force capable of protecting Australia's air and sea approaches and able to work with United States forces in periodic overseas coalition operations.

The importance of East Timor lies to a lesser extent in its demonstration that notions of a benign regional security environment could no longer be taken as a

---

[1] Overall, Australian defense spending declined from around 2.5 percent of the country's GNP in the mid-1980s to around 1.9 percent in 1999. (See Department of Defence, June 2000, p. 48; R. Smith, 2000, p. 468; "Dare We Hope for the ADF We Need?" 2000.)

given. More intrinsically, the crisis highlighted internal, low-intensity conflicts that would occur close to Australia's shores, rather than conventional inter-state wars and distant allied engagements, as the contingencies most likely to confront defense planners in the future—threat scenarios that had received only minor attention in ADF force planning and structuring.

The practical example of the INTERFET intervention underscored this state of affairs with Australia's defense planning in at least two respects:

- First, limited airlift and sealift capacities hindered the initial dispatch of Australian troops and hardware and, more important, obstructed the sub-sequent deployment of the logistical tail that is required to support forces once in the field. Indeed even relatively rudimentary tasks, such as pump-ing fuel oil directly from supply ships to dockside storage facilities, could not be undertaken due to a lack of appropriate equipment ("To Arms," 2001; "Pushing the Boundaries," 2000). Ultimately, it was the United States that had to be relied on to provide the bulk of these resources.

- Second, depleted ADF ranks meant that there was neither room for troop rotation nor the possibility of safeguarding against unexpected contingen-cies by maintaining a reserve force in a high state of combat readiness. As previously noted, had the INTERFET intervention lasted an additional few months or, more seriously, been contested by the TNI, the defense forces would have faced enormous and possibly insurmountable problems in sus-taining the operation, not the least in terms of relieving and replenishing personnel actively deployed on the ground (Cotton, 2000c; Bergin, 2000; Woodman, 2000).

These realizations came as a major shock to ADF planners and strategists, un-derscoring that a dramatic reformulation of the armed forces was urgently re-quired. In particular, they provided a compelling rationale for creating a new type of defense structure that would allow quick and decisive deployments to contain complex humanitarian emergency situations whenever they arose in or near Australia's principal areas of concern—the South Pacific and (to a lesser extent) Southeast Asia. The "blueprint" for achieving this long-run reconfigura-tion is provided by the country's most recent defense White Paper, titled *Defence 2000: Our Future Defence Force*, which was released by Canberra in December 2000 and is central to the discussion that appears in this chapter.

THE 2000 DEFENCE WHITE PAPER

The key strategic shift presented in the 2000 Defence White Paper is the re-duced focus on maintaining high-tech, conventional sea and air platforms and the increased attention paid to creating highly mobile land forces that can operate in defense of Australia as well as undertake lower-level missions in regional "hot spots." The aim of this strategy is to provide an army that is structured and resourced to ensure that a brigade-level contingent can be deployed on active duty for extended periods of time while maintaining at least a battalion group available for deployment elsewhere (Department of Defence, December 2000, p. xiii; "Enter the Cyber Warriors," 2000).

To achieve these goals, the size of the military is to be increased from 51,000 to 54,000 personnel by 2010. These personnel will be organized in six combat battalions and placed on at least a 90-day state of readiness, although the expectation is that most will be ready for deployment in 30 days or less. Supporting these troops will be a Special Operations Group (SOG) consisting of the current SAS Regiment and a high-readiness commando squad. In addition, the role of the Reserves is to be expanded to allow them to provide a more effective surge and sustainment capacity for regular army units.

Integral to these proposed goals will be new legislative provisions governing the use and employment of the Reserves, particularly with regard to levels and frequency of training and call-out procedures for active service. To support these ground troops, investments also will be made in several areas of combat hardware, including attack and transport helicopters, lightly armored mobility vehicles, amphibious resupply and support ships, thermal and tactical surveillance systems, and ground-based air defense assets (Department of Defence, December 2000, pp. 78–84; "To Arms," 2001; "Time to Mend Defence," 2000; "Day of the Digger," 2000; "A Change of Posture: No More Sitting on Defence," 2000; "Mobile Force in Army's Sights," 2000). To pay for these enhancements, the government has earmarked increased capital, personnel, and operating expenditures of $5 billion (Australian) over the next decade.

The strategic priorities for these reconfigured and expanded defense assets (and the ADF in general) are clearly spelled out in a hierarchical manner. First, the military is to ensure the defense of Australia and its direct approaches; second, foster the security of the country's immediate neighborhood in the Southwest Pacific; third, work with the ASEAN member states to promote stability and cooperation in Southeast Asia; fourth, contribute in appropriate ways to the maintenance of strategic stability in the wider Asia-Pacific region; and fifth, support the efforts of the international community, especially the United Nations, to uphold global security (Tow, 2001; Department of Defence, December 2000, pp. x, 29–31; "Matching Weapons to Region," 2000).

This delineated hierarchy is the first time that Canberra has attempted to prioritize among competing foreign and defense policy objectives and clearly places regional interests, especially those in Australia's immediate vicinity, over more-distant engagements. As Professor Stewart Woodman observes,

The White Paper makes it perfectly clear that Australia now prioritizes between regions and mission statements and that the Inner Arc is the main area of concern to the ADF. It further insinuates [through the notion of "appropriate" contributions] that it will probably only make token contributions to coalition operations that occur in distant Northeast Asian theaters—code for the Koreas and the Taiwan Straits (Woodman, 2000).

It should also be noted that whereas defending the Commonwealth is (quite justifiably) designated as the ADF's key mission, the White Paper makes the additional point that there are, presently, no credible state-based threats to Australia and that an attack on the mainland remains a distant possibility (Department of Defence, December 2000, pp. 23–24; "Canberra Beefs Up Military Strength," 2000). The unstated implication, therefore, is that Southeast Asia and especially the Southwest Pacific will constitute the Army's two main priorities, at least in terms of actual physical deployments.

Three salient questions flow from the 2000 White Paper: (1) Will it, in fact, provide a definitive blueprint for a newly reconfigured, highly mobile combat land force? (2) How does such a structure equate with Australia's wider Southeast Asian policy, particularly in light of regional concerns relating to Western interventionism? and (3) What are the implications of a more-discretely focused, less high-tech ADF for the U.S.-Australian defense relationship?

A DEFINITIVE BLUEPRINT FOR THE FUTURE?

John Howard has portrayed the 2000 Defence Review as "the most comprehensive reappraisal of Australian defence capability for decades," providing the country with the necessary means to address regional lower-level contingencies whenever they have an impact on the country's interests.[2] The general Australian policy and academic community has, likewise, endorsed the White Paper as a realistic and honest document that appropriately matches defense capacities to the types of contingencies most likely to confront the ADF in coming years (Bergin, 2000; Woodman, 2000).

To be sure, there are several ways in which the White Paper represents a major innovation in terms of Australian defense policy, particularly with respect to responding to complex, East Timor–like regional crises. The document, for instance,

- explicitly emphasizes the role of the Army in defending Australia's interests with specific reference to the ADF's use in low-tech, humanitarian-type operations

---

[2] Howard, cited in "Canberra Beefs Up Military Strength," 2000.

- recognizes the importance of investing in issues pertaining to logistical sustainment, tactical mobility, strategic lift, and troop rotation and preparedness

- underlines the basic point that Australia is more likely to be engaged in its own "backyard" than in more-distant theaters and, therefore, the defense forces need to be configured to meet contingencies most likely to arise in the local region

- affirms the importance of territorial self-reliance while acknowledging that a conventional attack on Australia remains highly improbable under current circumstances.

Nonetheless, a number of problems exist with the White Paper, which not only reflect a residual preoccupation with traditional defense postures but, more important, suggest a level of "schizophrenic" thinking in terms of long-term strategic planning. Perhaps the single most important issue in this regard is the inclusion of significant defense elements that continue to emphasize high-end, interoperable, and conventional capabilities.

Under the 2000 plan, the Navy will receive at least three state-of-the-art aircraft destroyers and new missile defenses and harpoon anti-ship missiles for the existing ANZAC surface fleet (although the overall number of combat frigates will be cut from 14 to 11).[3] Funding has also been earmarked for a substantial upgrade of six, long-range Collins class submarines, each of which will be refitted with modified, high-performance acoustic platforms and combat systems.

The Air Force will benefit from the purchase of 100 new fighters (which will eventually replace existing F/A-18 Hornets and F-111 bombers), five new-generation air-air refueling planes, and four Airborne Early Warning and Control craft, with the possibility of an additional three being purchased by 2010. Provision has also been made for the immediate upgrading of the F/A-18 fleet (it is expected that these aircraft will be gradually phased out of service as the new combat fighters come on line), including installations of advanced air-air missiles, tactical data links, and new helmet-mounted weapons cueing systems.

Finally, major expenditures have been slated for information warfare, including investments in intelligence, communications, and command; aerial spy planes (equipped with thermal surveillance systems); and an enhanced Jindalee Operational Network (JORN) to monitor Australia's northern approaches (Department of Defence, December 2000, pp. xiii–xv, 78–97; "To Arms," 2001;

---

[3]Original projections had called for the size of the combat fleet to be expanded to 16 frigates. (See "Chronicle of Strategic Decline," 2000.)

"Enter the Cyber Warriors," 2000; "Mobile Force in Army's Sights," 2000; "Time to Mend Defence," 2000; "Three New Warships Top Military Shopping List," 2000; "Day of the Digger," 2000).

It has been projected that at least $10.2 billion (U.S.) will have to be put aside to meet these various purchases and upgrades over the next ten years. This expenditure is justified on the grounds that an advanced air and naval combat capacity is of crucial importance in safeguarding Australia's maritime approaches (above and below) and is necessary in terms of keeping up with general Southeast Asian military acquisitions (Department of Defence, December 2000, pp. 84–85, 87–88, 97). The White Paper makes the additional point that, in the context of the Australian defense alliance with Washington, it is essential that these platforms achieve a high degree of integration and interoperability with U.S. assets. This strongly suggests continued future investments in RMA to ensure against "bloc obsolescence" (Woodman, 2000; Department of Defence, December 2000, pp. 34–35; R. Smith, 2000, p. 470).

These aspects of the White Paper are important in at least two respects:

- First, they raise the question of whether a decisive shift in defense policy has, in fact, actually taken place. Certainly emphasizing interoperability with the United States, conventional warfighting capacities, RMA, and protection of the air-sea gap bears a striking resemblance to strategic priorities highlighted in previous defense reviews. This type of force planning has little relevance to the type of lower-end operations that East Timor was supposed to represent (Monk, 2000b).[4] It is also worth noting that the combined capital expenditures for upgrading and modernizing air and sea assets is nearly $3 billion (U.S.) more than the amount that has been set aside for the Army. In absolute terms, therefore, the traditional emphasis on the Air Force and Navy remains in place (albeit to a lesser extent).

- Second, and more significant, aspects of the White Paper suggest a lack of direction in overall Australian defense policy. Investing in high-end capacities to augment territorial defense is at odds with the 2000 Review's repeated insistence that no credible (conventional) threat currently exists to the country. Similarly, the emphasis on interoperability in many ways conflicts with the strategic imperatives set out for the ADF, not the least because coalition engagements in distant theaters are accorded a low priority. Most important, structuring forces to enable coalition and/or conventional warfighting belies the rhetoric promoting a more-mobile, low-tech defense

---

[4]Similar sentiments were expressed by Professor William Tow during interviews at the University of Queensland, Brisbane, December 19, 2000.

capacity able to undertake "boots on the ground"–style operations and leaves unanswered the fundamental question of which way the ADF should be evolving: toward peacekeeping or RMA. The longer this central issue is sidelined, the more difficult it will be to address in a satisfactory manner (McFarlane, 2000).

Of course, it could be argued that the White Paper is simply trying to create a differential force structure that is capable of fulfilling both conventional and nonconventional missions. It is also true that high-tech assets such as signals intelligence (SIGINT) and air defenses can and often are used in defense of humanitarian and peacekeeping missions. As Anthony Bergin of the Australian Defence Studies Centre argues, "No government is going to commit ground forces where there is the possibility of escalation without the necessary hardware to protect them and respond in kind. The general rule in terms of military assets is that you go in with everything and then scale down. You never go in light and attempt to scale up" (Bergin, 2000). In these respects, therefore, the White Paper's emphasis on both low-end and high-end capabilities doesn't have to be seen as mutually exclusive and may not necessarily be a bad thing.

However, effectively achieving multitask defense capabilities of the sort described in this section necessitates both a sophisticated and lucid policy framework and, more important, money. As pointed out earlier, several contradictory themes underscore the 2000 Defence Review. These conflicting tendencies do not lend particularly strong support to the existence of the first requirement.

More problematic is the issue of finance. Assuming that all the White Paper's funding commitments are fulfilled and that projected future economic growth rates are met, by the end of the decade Australia will still be spending only 1.9 percent of its gross national product (GNP) on defense, roughly the same proportion as now (Monk, 2000b; "Chronicle of Strategic Decline," 2000). It is extremely unlikely that this level of defense spending will be sufficient to sustain a reliable high-end/low-end military structure that also keeps up with developments in RMA, and would be particularly true in the event of a significant drop in the value of the Australian dollar versus the U.S. greenback (Tow, 2000 and 2001).[5]

---

[5] Similar reservations were also expressed by Alan Dupont during interviews at the SDSC, ANU, Canberra, September 12, 2000.

THE 2000 DEFENCE WHITE PAPER AND AUSTRALIA'S WIDER SOUTHEAST ASIAN POLICY

As Chapter Three points out, John Howard's allusion to Australia acting as Washington's unilateral "deputy" in the wake of the East Timor intervention had a palpable impact on Canberra's wider relations in Southeast Asia, not the least in terms of galvanizing concerns about increased Western intervention-ism. These misgivings were aired not only by predictably "prickly" govern-ments—notably Kuala Lumpur and Jakarta—but also by erstwhile allies such as Thailand. References to a reconfigured military that is specifically designed to allow rapid deployments in areas of potential or actual unrest obviously carry important implications for heightening these regional perceptions, which could be detrimental to Australia's wider Southeast Asian engagement efforts.[6]

In an attempt to preclude an interventionist interpretation of Australia's future regional defense policy, the White Paper makes repeated references to Canberra's commitment to its immediate neighborhood and wider Southeast Asian theater and its desire to foster security, peace, and stability throughout the region. More important, it specifically rejects notions of unilateral interven-tion undertaken without the consent of the host government:

> Our planning needs to acknowledge that we could be called upon to undertake several [peacekeeping/enforcing and humanitarian] operations simultane-ously. . . . We would provide such support only at the request of a neighboring government. . . . We would also expect that other regional countries would pro-vide support, most probably in the form of a coalition operating under a UN or international mandate (Department of Defence, December 2000, pp. 48–49).

Inclusions such as these in the White Paper have certainly helped to ameliorate some of the concerns in Southeast Asia over possible Western-orchestrated interventionism, however only to a certain extent. As with the overall direction of ADF force structuring, ambiguity has clouded the clarity of the message being transmitted from Canberra. While the White Paper talks about regional cooperation, commitment, and confidence-building, it also alludes to the Southwest Pacific and (to a lesser extent) Southeast Asia as being the primary area of concern in terms of possible threats to Australian interests (R. Smith, 2000, p. 469).

In many ways, this dichotomy is indicative of the wider problem of how Australia actually views Asia: Should the region be regarded as a potentially hostile environment or an area to be engaged? The White Paper reflects both

---

[6]The irony here is that the East Timor crisis graphically illustrated the void in ASEAN's own force-projection capabilities. Had a more effective and reliable regional response mechanism been in place, there would now be less reason for Australia to develop rapidly deployable units of its own.

views without reconciling the inherent contradictions between them. More specifically, it fails to elucidate whether Canberra should be preparing its forces to meet threats originating from its immediate and near neighborhood, or whether it should configure the ADF so that it can be more readily integrated into wider Southeast Asian defense and security arrangements (Bergin, 2000; Woodman, 2000).

There is little doubt that the general uncertainty over Australia's foreign policy intentions has fed the overall climate of suspicion in Indonesia and Malaysia, both of which continue to express grave reservations over the possibility of future interventions being undertaken at the behest of Washington. Just as critically, the ambivalence in the White Paper has failed to fully dispel concerns in states such as Singapore and Vietnam, at least to the extent that there remains a general tendency to view Australia as a distant U.S. "satellite" that does not really belong to the region (Sebastian, 2000).

The existence of such lingering perceptions would be of lesser consequence had Australia not lost the support and backing of the former dominant state in Southeast Asia, Indonesia. However, now that the Canberra-Jakarta shared vision for the region has evaporated, it is vital that a more definitive policy line be established and communicated. The danger of not doing so will be to risk marginalization, and possibly full exclusion, from the established and budding institutions of Southeast Asian regionalism.

THE 2000 DEFENCE WHITE PAPER AND THE AUSTRALIAN-U.S. RELATIONSHIP

No other alliance in the Asia-Pacific comes even close to paralleling the Australian-U.S. defense partnership with its emphasis on shared values, mutual interests, and very special cooperative intelligence arrangements. Although the bond that tied the two countries together for much of the twentieth century— the common challenge and threat posed by the spread of Communism—has now disappeared, the bilateral alliance continues to offer substantial benefits to both parties.

For the United States, Australia reinforces America's strategic engagement in Asia and brings greater weight to policies aimed at preventing "rogue" states (for example, North Korea) from developing weapons of mass destruction, and augments efforts aimed at facilitating the spread of democracy, countering transnational security threats (such as the heroin trade), and promoting regional trade liberalization.

Washington also relies heavily on joint facilities in Australia for burden-sharing in the production of intelligence. Key among these is Pine Gap, which is located near Alice Springs and currently used as a spy satellite ground station by the Central Intelligence Agency (CIA) and National Reconnaissance Office (NRO) for monitoring arms control agreements and military developments in areas of strategic interest.

Finally, the United States has long counted on Canberra as an important "middle power diplomat" and regional crisis stabilizer with a unique knowledge of the South Pacific and general Southeast Asian area.[7] Certainly events in East Timor demonstrated the importance of being able to call on a reliable coalition partner to quickly initiate contingency measures capable of dampening sources of instability that may arise far from American shores (Baker and Paal, 2000, pp. 87–93; Albinski, 2000, pp. 555–567).

For Australia, the benefits of the alliance with the United States stem more from the role that Washington plays in maintaining order and stability in the Asia-Pacific, especially with regard to preventing a hostile hegemon or emergent great power from attaining strategic domination of East and/or Southeast Asia. In addition, Canberra's defense posture has profited significantly from the comprehensive, high-grade, and privileged intelligence that has arisen out of the various joint facility agreements that have been concluded with Washington. Without access to this shared information, Australia would not only be forced to invest in its own intelligence capability, it would also be deprived of the knowledge and understanding (gained through these contacts) that has proven to be so instrumental to the country's standing in a whole range of international environmental, economic, trade, and security forums (Baker and Paal, 2000, pp. 93–96).

Reflecting these various dimensions is the specific recognition that is accorded in the 2000 Defence Review to the centrality of the Australian-U.S. relationship:

> In 2001, Australia's formal alliance with the United States will reach 50 years of age with the anniversary of the signing of the ANZUS Treaty in September 1951. . . . The Treaty remains today the foundation of a relationship that is one of our great national assets. Since the end of the Cold War the United States and its allies have refashioned and reaffirmed their alliances to meet contemporary needs. As the Asia Pacific region has emerged as a focus of global security in the coming decades, so the U.S.-Australia alliance is as important to both parties today as it has ever been. . . . For Australia, continued U.S. engagement will support our defence capabilities and play a critical role in maintaining strategic stability in the region as a whole. For the United States, Australia is an important ally, a key partner in regional security efforts and a significant potential contributor to coalitions (Department of Defence, December 2000, p. 34).

---

[7] It should be noted that recent crises in the Solomons and Fiji have, arguably, undermined some of Australia's luster in this regard.

Overall, the United States has been highly receptive to the content and strategic thrust of Defence 2000. The recognized need for an ADF force structure that will enable Canberra to take the lead in regional interventions and make the commitment to allocate resources to maintain high-end, interoperable defense capacities accords well with the principal foreign policy goals of the current Bush administration. These priorities explicitly stress the need for reduced overseas American defense commitments and spending, emphasizing that allies must be prepared to buy more forcefully into the combined notions of coalition warfighting and burden-sharing as part of this need. The following remarks by Colin Powell, the newly appointed U.S. Secretary of State, during a Senate hearing in Washington in early 2001 were very much reflective of these sentiments:

> [W]e are very, very pleased that Australia . . . has displayed a keen interest in what's been happening in Indonesia [and the South Pacific]. And so we will coordinate our policies, but let our ally, Australia, take the lead as they have done so well in that troubled country [and part of the world].[8]

The White Paper's continued salience with regard to conventional warfighting assets and associated investments in the RMA, in particular, has garnered a favorable response from Washington. One of the greatest fears of the U.S. policy-making community was that Australia would follow the example set by New Zealand, whose own defense review in 2000 led to the institution of a massively pared-down force structure that was exclusively oriented to territorial self-defense and army-based peacekeeping and humanitarian missions.[9]

Had Australia adopted this model not only would it have precluded any possibility for contributions to wider coalition operations, it would also have effectively signaled that Canberra had abdicated all responsibility for moving and deploying its military (in terms of strategic sealifts and airlifts) to outside powers (U.S. State Department officials, 2000).

On a rhetorical level, therefore, Australian and U.S. interests would appear to coincide in terms of the substance of the 2000 Defence Review. If one takes a closer view, however, a number of difficulties become apparent. One problem is the extent to which Australia will actually be able to fulfill commitments to both high-end and low-end capabilities. As previously noted, budgetary financial constraints make it highly unlikely that the country will be able to achieve both

---

[8]Powell, quoted in "To Arms," 2001.

[9]Under the direction of New Zealand Prime Minister Helen Clark's Labour-Alliance, the government decided to retract from all planned naval, air-strike, and maritime surveillance expenditures, asserting that existing (air and sea) capacities would be used purely for territorial self-defense in the South Pacific (McFarlane, 2000; see also Ministry of Defence, New Zealand, 2000; Albinski, 2000, p. 555).

mandates simultaneously, at least in an effective manner. A fundamental conflict of interest is, therefore, likely to arise between meeting U.S. alliance commitments (such as making military assets available for patrol and surveillance duties in conflicts such as the Persian Gulf War of 1991) and freeing up resources for local contingencies, particularly if threats in the Inner Arc intensify to the point that concerted peacekeeping and enforcing duties are actually required (Tow, 2001).

In other words, Australia will probably become a more discriminating alliance partner, which, given the dictates of national interests that inevitably prioritize regional over global engagements, means the country will also potentially become a more difficult alliance partner.[10] This is particularly the case when one remembers that the Americans are only one group among others with whom Canberra's defense interactions need to be measured. The implication of New Zealand's current strategic posture is especially important in this regard. As noted earlier, Wellington's 2000 Defence Review resulted in the large-scale retraction of air- and sea-strike, surveillance, and lift capacities and the institution of a largely army-based peacekeeping force. Responsibility for the movement of these ground assets in the event of a major regional crisis will now, by default, almost certainly fall to the ADF. This will obviously have importance for Canberra's own defense spending, thinking, and prioritizing.

A second problem is the related point concerning the White Paper's allusion to "appropriate contributions," a reference that many Australian security analysts believe is indicative of a general unwillingness on the part of Canberra to back coalition operations with anything more than token provisions of support. As Professor William Tow observes, the mere fact that the size of the Navy's surface fleet is to be reduced from 14 vessels to 11 (notwithstanding the purchase of new aircraft destroyers) will have an impact on Australia's ability to act as an effective coalition partner in terms of open-water contingencies. Reflecting on this, Tow states, "The days when Canberra would willingly provide a couple of destroyers for coalition patrol duties at Washington's request are now clearly over" (Tow, 2001).

Indeed, it has been suggested that should a major conflict break out that requires the deployment of U.S. and allied forces, Canberra would probably be reluctant to commit *any* high-end assets for fear of losing them in the midst of battle-related hostilities (Bergin, 2000). A reticent stance of this type will almost

---

[10]This likelihood has been repeatedly raised by Professor Paul Dibb during various Parliamentary and Senate defense hearings held in 2001. Indeed, he maintains that the "die has probably already been cast" in terms of choosing between global and local priorities as the ADF cannot keep up with (U.S.-led) RMA and force modernization (due to budgetary constraints) and certainly cannot perform both a high-tech and low-tech role simultaneously.

certainly be rejected by the current Bush administration, which will want, and expect, to see Australia playing a far more decisive and active role.[11]

A third difficulty revolves around defense funding. Ensuring that conventional air and sea platforms remain compatible with U.S. equipment will require committing to a significant and ongoing investment in RMA. It has been estimated that the full cost of this expenditure could run as much as $80 to $100 billion (U.S.) over the next five to ten years (McFarlane, 2000). These dollar figures are far in excess of the $10 billion (U.S.) that has been set aside in the White Paper to finance conventional defense upgrades and purchases. How such excess spending will actually be met is an issue that the Australian defense and policymaking community has yet to adequately consider, much less definitively address (Woodman, 2000).[12]

Perhaps most problematic, however, is the issue of perceptions. Because of the broadly inclusive way that the White Paper has been written, a growing assumption has arisen in Washington that Canberra is able and willing to take the lead in regional contingencies as well as fulfill a concerted-alliance role in more distant theaters. The United States' supreme military commander in the Pacific, Admiral Dennis Blair, has already hinted as much. Indeed, after being briefed on the contents of the Defence 2000 White Paper, he voiced confidence that it would now, hopefully, be less difficult than it was in the past for Australia to maintain operations both in its own neighborhood and alongside the United States in extraregional conflicts ("Fight with Us, US Admiral Tells Defence Chiefs," 2000). As has been pointed out throughout this chapter, such expectations remain at significant odds with the reality of Australian defense capabilities, particularly over the medium to long term when issues of finance are likely to have an increasingly decisive impact.

Further coloring the "strategic perception" equation is Pine Gap and the role Washington expects it to play in its planned national missile defense (NMD) system. Although not specifically mentioned in the 2000 White Paper, the document's affirmation of the centrality of the Australian-U.S. alliance has certainly encouraged American defense planners to assume Canberra will allow modification of the Alice Springs facility to provide early-warning confirmation of a ballistic missile attack on the U.S. mainland. This reasoning is by no means axiomatic, however.

---

[11]This is particularly true in terms of assuming the mantle for security and stability along the Asia-Pacific's southern rim.

[12]Similar views were expressed by William Tow at the University of Queensland, Brisbane, on December 19, 2000, and March 6, 2001.

The Labor Opposition of Australia's Labor Party leader Kim Beazley, which looks set to win the next general election (which must be called in 2001), is on record as opposing the integration of Pine Gap into a proposed NMD system on the grounds that it would damage both international stability and wider disarmament efforts. Moreover, there remains an active concern that endorsing and participating in American antiballistic defenses will inevitably serve to antagonize China[13] and prompt Beijing to adopt a largely obstructive stance vis-à-vis Australia's regional Asian engagement efforts (Tow, 2001). China has already accused the current Howard administration of being an American "cat's paw" for indicating an "understanding" of Washington's position on NMD and has warned of serious setbacks to bilateral relations should Australia decide to participate more fully in missile defenses (Albinski, 2000, p. 553; Moore, 2000; Shaube, 2000; "PRC Likely to Increase Pressure on Australia for Backing US NMD," 2000). Encapsulating these concerns, shadow Foreign Minister Laurie Brereton has decried NMD as a "thoroughly unhelpful development" and affirmed that "Labour in office would very closely review any involvement by Australia" in such a system.[14]

Should Australia, in fact, deny modification of Pine Gap for NMD purposes, it will significantly complicate bilateral relations and could well prompt Washington to adopt an increasingly hard line against Canberra, possibly as an example to other alliance partners (such as France) who are similarly opposed to NMD. In the words of William Tow, "It is far easier for the U.S. to push Australia around than other European allies. Between January/February 2002 and mid-year, you are undoubtedly going to see increasingly hard discussions between Washington and Canberra over Pine Gap; it is going to become a hot issue" (Tow, 2001; Albinski, 2000, p. 556).

Australian-U.S. relations thus appear to be set for a somewhat uncertain and possibly tumultuous period over the next few years. The nature of the future bilateral defense partnership will very much depend on developments in Canberra's regional strategic environment and the extent to which the government will be forced into making fundamental choices between global high-end and regional low-end priorities. Just as important will be the degree of dependency that is built into the U.S.-Australian alliance and the extent to which Canberra is prepared to pursue strategic ties with Washington for the sake of wider regional relationships in the Asia-Pacific.

---

[13]China has come out strongly against NMD on the grounds that it will both neutralize its own small intercontinental arsenal and spark a new, destabilizing nuclear arms race in Asia. (See, for instance, Albinski, 2000, p. 546.)

[14]Brereton, cited in "Australia Could Become a NMD Target," 2000.

If Defence 2000 is to act as a truly definitive blueprint for Australia's future military and external needs, it is vital that the various contradictions and tensions inherent in its substance are addressed. The White Paper, as currently configured, remains extremely open-ended and subject to wide interpretation—attempting, in essence, to be something for everybody. Although this may be good public policy in terms of generating multipartisan backing and endorsement, it provides neither a consistent, nor indeed a coherent, basis for long-term defense and foreign policy planning, structuring, or prioritizing (Woodman, 2000).

The ambiguous nature of the Defence 2000 Review has created the danger that a resource-deprived differential force structure will be created that is lacking at both the high end and the low end of the defense spectrum. In addition, the document has fed into a somewhat obfuscated Southeast Asian policy and generated largely unfounded expectations of what Canberra is able (or willing) to bring to the table in terms of U.S. alliance commitments and contributions. Such a state of affairs is hardly suited to the rigors that Australia will face as it enters what may well turn out to be one of the most challenging and unpredictable eras that has faced the government since the country's attainment of nationhood in 1901.

BIBLIOGRAPHY

BOOKS AND BOOK CHAPTERS

Aditjondro, G., *In the Shadow of Mount Ramelau: The Impact of the Occupation of East Timor*, Den Haag, The Netherlands: CID, 1994.

Baker, John, and Douglas Paal, "The US-Australia Alliance," in Robert Blackwell and Paul Dibb, eds., *America's Asian Alliances*, Cambridge, Mass.: MIT Press, 2000.

Ball, Desmond, and Hamish McDonald, *Death in Balibo, Lies in Canberra*, Sydney: Allen and Unwin, 2000.

Brown, Gary, Frank Frost, and Stephen Sherlock, *The Australian-Indonesian Security Agreement: Issues and Implications*, Canberra: Department of the Parliamentary Library, Parliamentary Research Service, 1996.

Catley, Bob, and Visesio Dugis, *Australian and Indonesian Relations Since 1945: The Garuda and the Kangaroo*, Aldershot, England: Ashgate Publishing, 1998.

Chalk, Peter, *Non-Military Security and Global Order: The Impact of Violence, Chaos and Extremism on National and International Security*, London: Macmillan, 2000a.

Cotton, James, "East Timor and Australia—Twenty-Five Years of the Policy Debate," in James Cotton, ed., *East Timor and Australia*, Canberra: Australian Defence Studies Centre, 2000a.

Cotton, James, and John Ravenhill, "Australia's Engagement with Asia," in James Cotton and John Ravenhill, eds., *Seeking Asian Engagement: Australia in World Affairs, 1991–95*, Melbourne: Oxford University Press, 1997.

Dunn, James, "Portuguese Timor: The Independence Movement from Coalition to Cooperation," in James Cotton, ed., *East Timor and Australia*, Canberra: Australian Defence Studies Centre, 2000.

_____, *Timor: A People Betrayed*, Milton, Queensland: Jacaranda Press, 1983.

Evans, Gareth, and Bruce Grant, *Australia's Foreign Relations in the World of the 1990s*, Melbourne: Melbourne University Press, 1995.

Firth, Stewart, *Australia in International Politics*, Sydney: Allen and Unwin, 1999.

Frost, Frank, *Australia's War in Vietnam*, Sydney: Allen and Unwin, 1987.

Gelber, H. G., *The Australian-American Alliance: Costs and Benefits*, London: Penguin Books, 1968.

George, Margaret, *Australia and the Indonesian Revolution*, Melbourne: Melbourne University Press, 1980.

Goldsworthy, David, "Australia and Good International Citizenship," in Stephanie Lawson, ed., *The New Agenda for Global Security: Cooperating for Peace and Beyond*, Sydney: Allen and Unwin, 1995.

Grey, Jeffrey, *A Military History of Australia*, Cambridge, Mass.: MIT Press, 1999.

Harris, Stuart, "Australia and the International Environment," in James Cotton and John Ravenhill, eds., *Seeking Asian Engagement: Australia in World Affairs, 1991–95*, Melbourne: Oxford University Press, 1997.

Hastings, Peter, "The Timor Problem," in James Cotton, ed., *East Timor and Australia*, Canberra: Australian Defence Studies Centre, 2000.

Hill, H., "The Economy," in H. Hill, ed., *Indonesia's New Order: The Dynamics of Socio-Economic Transformation*, Sydney: Allen and Unwin, 1994.

Keating, Paul, *Engagement: Australia Faces the Pacific*, Sydney: Macmillan, 2000.

Langfield, Michele, "Bridging the Cultural Divide: Movements of People Between Australia and Asia," in Mark McGillivray and Gary Smith, eds., *Australia and Asia*, Melbourne: Oxford University Press, 1997.

Legge, J., *Sukarno: A Political Biography*, Sydney: Allen and Unwin, 1984.

Leifer, Michael, *Dictionary of the Modern Politics of Southeast Asia*, London: Routledge, 1996.

MacIntyre, Andrew, "Comprehensive Engagement and Australian Security Interests in Southeast Asia," in Greg Fry, ed., *Australia's Regional Security*, Sydney: Allen and Unwin, 1991.

Mackie, Jamie, "Australia and Indonesia, 1945–60," in G. Greenwood and N. Harper, eds., *Australia in World Affairs, 1956–60*, Melbourne: Melbourne University Press, 1963.

_____, "The Politics of Asian Immigration," in James Coughlin and Deborah McNamara, eds., *Asians in Australia*, London: Macmillan, 1997.

Maley, Michael, "Reflections on the Peace Process in Cambodia," in Hugh Smith, ed., *Peacekeeping: Challenges for the Future*, Canberra: Australian Defence Force Academy, 1993.

Manning, Robert, "Security in East Asia," in William Carpenter and David Wiencek, eds., *Asian Security Handbook: An Assessment of Political-Security Issues in the Asia Pacific Region*, New York: M. E. Sharpe, 1996.

McDougall, Derek, *Australia's Foreign Relations*, Melbourne: Longman, 1998.

Meaney, Neville, *Australia and the World: A Documentary History from the 1870s to the 1970s*, Melbourne: Longman Cheshire, 1985.

Mediansky, Fedor, "The Development of Australian Foreign Policy," in P. Boyce and J. Angel, eds., *Diplomacy in the Market Place: Australia in World Affairs, 1981–90*, Melbourne: Longman Cheshire, 1992.

Menon, Jayant, "Australia-Asia Economic Diplomacy: Regional Economic Diplomacy in the Asia-Pacific," in Mark McGillivray and Gary Smith, eds., *Australia and Asia*, Melbourne: Oxford University Press, 1997.

Millar, T., *Australia in Peace and War: External Relations, 1788–1977*, New York: St. Martin's Press, 1978.

Schwarz, Adam, *Indonesia: A Nation in Waiting*, Sydney: Allen and Unwin, 1994.

Sheridan, Greg, "Australia's Asian Odyssey," in Greg Sheridan, ed., *Living with Dragons, Australia Confronts its Asian Destiny*, Sydney: Allen and Unwin, 1995.

Smith, Gary, Dave Cox, and Scott Burchill, *Australia in the World*, Melbourne: Oxford University Press, 1997.

Viviani, Nancy, "Australia and Southeast Asia," in James Cotton and John Ravenhill, eds., *Seeking Asian Engagement: Australia in World Affairs, 1991–95*, Melbourne: Oxford University Press, 1997.

Walters, Patrick, "Australia and Indonesia," in Mark McGillivray and Gary Smith, eds., *Australia and Asia*, Melbourne: Oxford University Press, 1997.

Whitlam, Gough, "Australia, Indonesia and Europe's Empires," in James Cotton, ed., *East Timor and Australia*, Canberra: Australian Defence Studies Centre, 2000.

OFFICIAL REPORTS AND GOVERNMENT DOCUMENTS

Barwick, Garfield, address to the Australian Institute of Political Science, January 1964, cited in Patrick Walters, "Australia and Indonesia," in Mark McGillivray and Gary Smith, eds., *Australia and Asia*, Melbourne: Oxford University Press, 1997.

Chomsky, Noam, untitled statement delivered to the Fourth Committee of the United Nations Generally Assembly, November 1978.

Crouch, Harold, "East Timor Hearings," *Senate Foreign Affairs, Defence, and Trade References Committee Hansard*, September 20, 1999.

Department of Defence, *Defence Review 2000—Our Future Defence Force: A Public Discussion Paper,* Canberra: Department of Defence, June 2000.

_____, *Defence 2000: Our Future Defence Force,* Canberra: Department of Defence, December 2000.

Department of Information, *Indonesia 1996: An Official Handbook,* Jakarta: Department of Information, Republic of Indonesia, 1996.

Downer, Alexander, "Australia's Future in the Asia Pacific: Cooperation, Economic Reform and Liberalisation," speech given before the Melbourne Institute Conference—The Asian Crisis—Economic Analysis and Market Intelligence, University of Melbourne, May 8, 1998 (accessed via http://www.dfat.gov.au).

_____, "Australia—Stability in the Asia Pacific," address to the Australian-American Association, Harvard Club, New York, June 8, 1998 (accessed via http://www.dfat.gov.au).

"East Timor Hearings," *The Senate Foreign Affairs, Defence, and Trade References Committee Hansard*, September, 20 1999.

_____, *The Senate Foreign Affairs, Defence and Trade References Committee Hansard*, November 4, 1999.

_____, *The Senate Foreign Affairs, Defence and Trade References Committee Hansard*, November 11, 1999.

East Timor: Report of the Senate Foreign Affairs, Defence and Trade References Committee, Canberra: Australian Senate, November 11, 1999.

Evans, Gareth, *Australia's Regional Security, Ministerial Statement by the Minister for Foreign Affairs and Trade,* Canberra: Government Publishing Service, 1989.

Ministry of Defence, New Zealand, *The Government's Defence Policy Framework,* Wellington: Ministry of Defence, June 2000.

Scrafton, Michael, "East Timor Hearings," *Senate Foreign Affairs, Defence and Trade References Committee Hansard*, November 11, 1999.

White, Hugh, Deputy Secretary (Strategy), Department of Defence, "Estimate Hearings," *Legislation Committee Hansard*, May 3, 2000.

JOURNAL ARTICLES AND MONOGRAPHS

Albinski, Henry, "Issues in Australian Foreign Policy," *The Australian Journal of Politics and History*, Vol. 46, No. 4, 2000.

Aspinall, Ed, "Whither Aceh?" *Inside Indonesia*, April–June 2000.

Ball, Desmond, "Arms and Affluence: Military Acquisitions in the Asia Pacific Region," *International Security*, Winter 1993/94.

Bergin, Anthony, "The Australian-Indonesian Timor Gap Maritime Boundary Agreement," *International Journal of Estuarine and Coastal Law*, Vol. 5, 1990.

Brown, Geoffrey, "Attitudes to an Invasion of Australia in 1942," *Journal of the Royal United Services Institute of Defence Studies*, March 1977.

Chopra, Jarat, "The UN's Kingdom of East Timor," *Survival*, Vol. 42, No. 3, 2000.

Collison, Kerry, "Indonesia: Disintegration of the Last Great Colonial Power?" *Defense and Foreign Affairs Strategic Policy*, Vol. XXVIII, No. 10, 2000.

Cotton, James, "The Emergence of an Independent East Timor: National and Regional Challenges," *Contemporary Southeast Asia*, Vol. 22, No. 1, 2000b.

_____, "Peacekeeping in East Timor: An Australian Policy Departure," *The Australian Journal of International Affairs*, Vol. 53, No. 3, 1999.

Downer, Alexander, "East Timor—Looking Back on 1999," *Australian Journal of International Affairs*, Vol. 54, No. 1, 2000.

Dupont, Alan, "ASEAN's Response to the East Timor Crisis," *Australian Journal of International Affairs*, Vol. 54, No. 2, 2000a.

_____, "The Australia-Indonesia Security Arrangement," *Australian Quarterly*, Vol. 68, No. 2, 1996.

_____, "East Timor's Future: Penury or Prosperity?" *Pacifica Review*, Vol. 12, No. 1, 2000b.

_____, "Unregulated Population Flows in East Asia: A New Security Problem," *Pacifica Review*, Vol. 9, No. 1, 1997.

Emerson, Donald, "Will Indonesia Survive?" *Foreign Affairs*, May/June 2000, pp. 103–104.

Frost, Frank, "The Peace Process in Cambodia," *Adelphi Papers*, No. 69, 1993.

Henderson, Donald, "Moralpolitik: The Timor Test," *The National Interest*, Vol. 58, Winter 1999/2000.

Huntley, Wade, and Peter Haysel, "East Timor and Asian Security," *Bulletin of Concerned Asian Scholars*, Vol. 31, Nos. 1–2, 2000.

Jones, David, and Michael Smith, "Advance Australia— Anywhere," *Orbis*, Vol. 43, No. 3, Summer 1999.

Lowry, B., "Australia-Indonesia Security Cooperation: For Better or Worse?" Strategic Defence and Studies Centre Working Paper, No. 299, 1996.

Maley, William, "The UN and East Timor," *Pacifica Review*, Vol. 12, No. 1, February 2001.

Milner, Anthony, "What Is Left of Engagement with Asia?" *The Australian Journal of International Affairs*, Vol. 54, No. 2, 2000.

O'Neill, Robert, "Australian Defence Policy Under Labour," *Journal of the Royal United Services Institute for Defence Studies*, September 1973.

Ravich, Samantha, "Eyeing Indonesia Through the Lens of Aceh," *The Washington Quarterly*, Vol. 23, No. 3, 2000.

Salla, Michael, "Australian Foreign Policy and East Timor," *Australian Journal of International Affairs*, Vol. 49, No. 2, November 1995.

Singh, Udai, "East Timor: Pebble in Indonesia's Shoe," *Strategic Analysis, Vol. XIX*, No. 9, 1996.

Smith, Gary, "Perspectives on Australian Foreign Policy, 1998," *Australian Journal of International Affairs*, Vol. 53, No. 2, 1999.

Smith, Roy, "The Unwieldy Sword of Justice: Australia's Defence Review and Regional Security Issues," *Security Dialogue*, Vol. 31, No. 4, 2000.

Stokes, Geoffrey, "Australians as Global Citizens: A Review," *Curriculum Corporation*, 1996.

Tiwon, Sylvia, "From Heroes to Rebels," *Inside Indonesia*, April–June 2000.

NEWSPAPER ARTICLES, NEWSLETTERS, CONFERENCE PAPERS, CURRENT AFFAIRS BULLETINS, AND UNPUBLISHED PAPERS

"$26m Fund for Timor Rebel Force," *The Australian*, November 24, 2000.

"Ambivalence Serves Only to Marginalise Us," *The Australian*, October 30, 1996.

"Anger in Asia as Australia Searches for New Regional Role," *Associated Press*, France, September 26, 1999.

"As Timor Smolders, Australia Expands Its Role," *The International Herald Tribune*, May 6, 1999.

"Asian Media Criticizes Australia's Role in East Timor," *Asia Pulse*, September 29, 1999.

"Aust. Cancels Military Training with Indonesia," *Associated Press*, September 10, 1999.

"Australia Could Become a NMD Target," *South Melbourne News*, July 18, 2000.

"Australia Must Know Its Place," *The New Straits Times*, May 23, 2000.

"Australia Risks Being on the Outer in Asia," *The Australian*, December 6, 2000.

"Australia Sees Reason," *The Economist*, July 7, 2001.

"Australia Targets the Boat People," *The Age*, November 15, 2000.

"Australian Defence Policy Under Labor," *Journal of the Royal United Services Institute for Defence Studies*, September 1973.

"Australia's Acid Test at the Bottom of the Timor Sea," *The Australian Financial Review*, October 14, 2000.

"Canberra Beefs Up Military Strength," *The Bangkok Post*, December 7, 2000.

"A Case of Regional Identity," *The Australian*, November 1, 1996.

Chalk, Peter, "Aceh: Indonesia's Continuing Headache," *Jane's Terrorism and Security Monitor*, December 2000b.

"A Change of Posture: No More Sitting on Defence," *The Sydney Morning Herald*, December 7, 2000.

"Chronicle of Strategic Decline," *The Australian*, December 7, 2000.

"Dare We Hope for the ADF We Need?" *The Age*, November 13, 2000.

"Day of the Digger," *The Sydney Morning Herald*, December 7, 2000.

"Defence Shift Is Overstated," *The Australian*, April 12, 2000.

"Democracy Marred by Mayhem." *The Australian*, September 13, 1999.

Djalal, Dini, "A Bloody Truce," *The Far Eastern Economic Review*, October 5, 2000.

Dolven, Ben, "A Rising Drum Beat," *The Far Eastern Economic Review*, November 16, 2000.

"Downer Should Be a Realist," *The Australian Financial Review*, August 14, 2000.

Dupont, Alan, "Indonesia, Australia and the Problem of East Timor," *AUS-CSCAP Newsletter*, Vol. 8, 1999.

"E. Timor Rivals Plan for War, Peace," *The Washington Post*, August 25, 1999.

"The East Timor Crisis," *Strategic Comments*, Vol. 5, No. 8, 1999.

"East Timor Crisis Heralds Change in ASEAN and Regional Power Struggles," *Associated Press*, September 26, 1999.

"East Timor to Raise Army," *The Border Mail*, November 24, 2000.

"Economy of Scale," *The Far Eastern Economic Review*, February 11, 1999.

"Enter the Cyber Warriors," *The Australian*, December 7, 2000.

"Facing Up to a Shameful Past," *The Age*, September 14, 2000.

"Fight with Us, US Admiral Tells Defence Chiefs," *The Sydney Morning Herald*, November 17, 2000.

"Fixed Relations," *The Weekend Australian*, March 15–16, 1997.

"Guilty as Charged: The East Timor Verdict," *The Age*, December 20, 2000.

"Gun Attack on Embassy," *The Age*, September 22, 1999.

"History Binds Indonesia and Australia," *The Jakarta Post*, October 13, 1999.

"How the PM Has Been Working Overtime to Forge Asian Link," *The Australian*, December 12, 1995.

"Howard Faces Dilemma on E. Timor," *The Jakarta Post*, March 8, 1999.

"Howard Sets Back RI-Canberra Ties," *The Jakarta Post*, December 9, 1999.

"Howard Still Under Fire over Regional Policy," *Asia Pulse*, September 29, 1999.

"Howardism," *The Indonesian National News Agency*, December 19, 1999.

"Human Rights and Pro-Independence Actions in Papua, 1999–2000," *Human Rights Watch*, Vol. 12, No. 2, 2000.

"Indonesia Asks for UN Force to Calm E. Timor," *Los Angeles Times*, September 13, 1999.

"Indonesia-Australia Ties: What Went Wrong?" *The Jakarta Post*, December 1, 1999.

"Indonesia Cancels Canberra Meeting," *The Canberra Times*, October 25, 2000.

"Indonesia Is in Danger of Coming Apart," *The Australian*, August 12, 2000.

"Indonesia Scraps Security Treaty over East Timor," *Associated Press*, Australia, September 16, 1999.

"Indonesian Defence Ties Helped in Timor Crisis," *Associated Press*, May 3, 2000.

"Indonesian President Voted Out," *The Washington Post*, July 24, 2001.

"Indonesian Protesters Attack Australian Ambassador," *The Sydney Morning Herald*, November 22, 2000.

"It's a Blow to Lose the Pact We Had to Have," *The Australian*, September 17, 1999.

"It's Time for Timor," *The Sydney Morning Herald*, January 30, 1999.

"Jakarta Severs Security Ties with Canberra," *The Australian*, September 17, 1999.

"Jakarta's Simmering Anger over Timor," *The Australian Financial Review*, August 10, 2000.

"Jakarta Snub Reflects Our Poor Relations," *The Australian*, October 25, 2000.

"The Keating Files," *The Australian*, March 13, 2000.

Klitgaard, Robert, "Unsolicited Thoughts on Helping East Timor Succeed," unpublished briefing paper, RAND Graduate School, Santa Monica, Calif., February 4, 2001.

"Leadership Team Hailed as Vital Step," *The Sydney Morning Herald*, July 15, 2000.

"Main Players Duck for Cover over Timor," *The Sydney Morning Herald*, September 14, 2000.

"Matching Weapons to Region," *The Australian*, December 7, 2000.

McFarlane, John, and William Maley, "Civilian Police in United Nations Peace Operations: Some Lessons from Recent Australian Experience," paper presented before the Ninth Meeting of the Council for Security Cooperation in the Asia Pacific (CSCAP), Working Group on Transnational Crime, Sydney, May 8–9, 2001.

"Megawati Makes Her Move," *The Economist*, June 2, 2001.

"Militia Leader Will Be Quizzed on Dili," *The Advertiser*, September 12, 2000.

"Militia Thug Eurico Guterres Leads a Charmed Life," *The Age*, September 27, 2000.

"Misjudgments Will Hurt Us Too," *The Australian*, September 10, 1999.

"Mobile Force in Army's Sights," *The Australian*, December 7, 2000.

Monk, Paul, "A Slippery Slope to Complicity: Australian Policy on Portuguese Timor: 1963–76. As Revealed by the National Archives," unpublished paper, December 2000a.

Murphy, Dan, "Irian Jaya: The Next Headache," *The Far Eastern Economic Review*, April 29, 2000.

"New Military Ties with Indonesia in Sight," *The Canberra Times*, December 11, 2000.

"Partnerships the Cornerstone of Defence," *The Australian*, September 22, 1999.

"Pattern of Dangerous Escalation Takes Hold," *The Australian Financial Review*, September 17, 1999.

"Perky Future," *The Far Eastern Economic Review*, February 18, 1999.

"PM Puts Premium on Political Stability," *The Australian Financial Review*, March 23, 1992.

"PRC Likely to Increase Pressure on Australia for Backing US NMD," *Today's Australia*, August 8, 2000.

"Pushing the Boundaries," *The Sydney Morning Herald*, December 15, 2000.

"Rebel Says Australian Stance a Terrible Mistake," *The Sydney Morning Herald*, December 15, 2000.

"A Rude Awakening: We're On Our Own," *The Age*, November 9, 1999.

Shaube, John, "Commentary," *The Sydney Morning Herald*, July 26, 2000.

"Square One," *Washington Post*, March 29, 2000.

Sulong, Sri Zainal Abidin, "The Regional Impact and the Role of the Region in Indonesia's Transformation," paper presented before the Council for Security Cooperation in the Asia Pacific (CSCAP) Indonesia's Future Challenges and Implications for the Region Seminar, Jakarta, March 8–9, 2000.

"Supporters Out in Force as Guterres Appears in Court," *The Australian Financial Review*, January 3, 2001.

"Talking About a Devolution," *The Economist*, January 6, 2001.

"Thousands Flee Homes in E. Timor," *The Washington Post*, July 20, 1999.

"Three New Warships Top Military Shopping List," *The Kalgoorie Miner*, December 12, 2000.

"Ties with Indonesian Military Prevented Bloodshed: Cosgrove," *Canberra Times*, May 17, 2000.

"Time to Mend Defence," *The Herald Sun*, December 9, 2000.

"Timor Tragedy Files Revealed Today," *The Sydney Morning Herald*, September 12, 2000.

"Timor's Troubled Waters," *The Economist*, December 2, 2000.

"To Arms," *The Economist*, February 3, 2001.

"UN Plans for E. Timor Authority," *The Washington Post*, September 16, 1999.

"UN Security Council Approves East Timor Force," *Los Angeles Times*, September 15, 1999.

"Violence-Torn E. Timor Put Under Martial Law," *The Washington Post*, September 7, 1999.

"We Won't Judge Timor Action: PM," *The Age*, September 14, 2000.

"We're Solid in a Crisis," *The Australian*, April 27, 1998.

"When Change Calls for Consistency," *The Australian*, October 30, 1996.

"Will Our Defence Dollars Be Enough?" *The Sydney Morning Herald*, December 12, 2000.

INTERVIEWS AND COMMENTS

Australian government officials and regional Indonesian academics and country experts, Jakarta, Singapore, and Canberra, October and December 2000.

Barton, Greg, Melbourne Hyatt, Melbourne, December 18, 2000.

Bergin, Anthony, Australian Defence Force Academy (ADFA), Canberra, December 15, 2000.

Cotton, James, Australian Defence Force Academy (ADFA), Canberra, December 14, 2000c.

Defense officials, Australian Embassy, Jakarta, October 16, 2000.

_____, Department of Defence, Canberra, December 15, 2000.

Dupont, Alan, Strategic and Defence Studies Centre (SDSC), Canberra, September 12, 2000c.

Foreign and political affairs officials, Australian Embassy, Washington, D.C., September 20, 2000.

Indonesian security analysts, Center for Political and Area Studies, Indonesian Institute of Sciences (PPW-LIPI), Jakarta, October 16, 2000.

Indonesian foreign affairs experts, U.S. Embassy, Jakarta, October 16–17, 2000.

Kadir, Suzaine, National University of Singapore (NUS), Singapore, October 19, 2000.

Mandane, Brigadier Jeanne (retired), comments during the Ninth Meeting of the Council for Security Cooperation in the Asia Pacific (CSCAP), Working Group on Transnational Crime, Sydney, Australia, May 8–9, 2001.

McFarlane, John, RAND, Virginia, September 22, 2000.

_____, comments made during the Ninth Meeting of the Council for Security Cooperation in the Asia Pacific (CSCAP) Working Group on Transnational Crime, Sydney, Australia, May 8–9, 2001.

Monk, Paul, Melbourne Hyatt, Melbourne, December 18, 2000b.

Moore, John, Australian Defence Minister, transcript of press conference, Canberra, July 22, 2000.

Mull, Steven, U.S. Embassy, Jakarta, October 17, 2000.

Sebastian, Leonard, Institute for Defense and Strategic Studies (IDSS), Singapore, October 18, 2000.

Security and foreign affairs analysts, Center for Political and Area Studies, Indonesian Institute of Sciences (PPW-LIPI), October 16, 2000.

_____, Research Institute for Democracy and Peace (RIDeP), Jakarta, October 16, 2000.

Thayer, Caryle, Asia Pacific Center for Security Studies (APCSS), Honolulu, Hawaii, August 10, 2000.

Tow, William, University of Queensland, Brisbane, December 19, 2000, and March 6, 2001.

U.S. State Department officials, U.S. State Department, Washington, D.C., September 20, 2000.

Woodman, Stewart, Australian Defence Force Academy (ADFA), Canberra, December 15, 2000.